DISCIPLESHIP FOUNDATIONS

STEP ONE - SALVATION

DR. HENDRIK J. VORSTER

TEACHER MANUAL

CONTENTS

Great Commission   v

Introduction   vii

PART I
REPENTANCE FROM DEAD WORK
Assimilation Sheet   11

PART II
FAITH IN GOD
Assimilation Sheet   27

How can I be Born Again?   29

PART III
BAPTISMS
Assimilation Sheet   67

PART IV
LAYING ON OF HANDS
Assimilation Sheet   75

PART V
THE RESURRECTION OF THE DEAD.
Assimilation Sheet   83

PART VI
ETERNAL JUDGMENT
Assimilation Sheet   91

PART VII
Conclusion on the six Foundational Principles: 93

Other Books of Dr. Hendrik J Vorster   95

Discipleship Foundations Series

Step 1 – Salvation (Teacher Manual)

By Dr. Hendrik J. Vorster

A practical guide to being a good disciple of Lord Jesus Christ

Apart from this Handbook, you will also need the following items to complete your study:

New International Version, of the Bible.
A pen or pencil to write the answers.
Coloured pencils (red, blue, green and yellow).

For more copies and information please visit and write to us at:
www.churchplantinginstitute.com
resources@churchplantinginstitute.com

ISBN 978-1-7338266-4-8

GREAT COMMISSION

"... 19 Go therefore and make disciples of all the nations, baptizing them
..., 20 teaching them to observe all things that I have commanded
you; and ..., I am with you always, even to the end of the age."
Matthew 28:18-20 (NKJV)

INTRODUCTION

The Christian Faith is about people putting their Faith in Jesus Christ as their Saviour and to follow Him as His first Disciples did. The Christian Faith is about being born again. It is about confession and receiving forgiveness for your sins. It is about becoming a child of God. It is about becoming part of the family of God as His son and daughter. It is about becoming a citizen of the Kingdom of God. It is about being restored, finding your purpose in life, and ultimately finding and fulfilling God's purpose for your life.

To be a part of this Kingdom of God requires us to bow our knees and confess our sins and accept Jesus Christ as our Lord and Saviour. This course is designed to help people give their lives to the Lord, or, for those who made a decision for Christ but never put down roots for their faith grow, to affirm their faith in Jesus and finally to put down roots and grow to maturity in Christ. Whichever one you might be, I pray that the Lord would use this material to guide you to an enriching experience with living in fellowship and on purpose for God.

This course is based on the Bible

This course is built on the Bible and therefor you will find a lot of Scriptures in it. Scriptures are paragraphs or sentences from the various Books of the Bible. The Bible is a combination of 66 Books. The first part of the Bible is called the ***"Old Testament"*** and contains the writings of various Servants of God. The Old Testament help us understand the Nature of God, but also help us understand the principles and purpose of God for our lives. The ***"New Testament"*** contains the history of Jesus' coming to earth, His earthly ministry, and then the various letters from some of the Servants of God to some of the Churches which was planted as a result of this newly found faith in Jesus Christ. The latter contain incredible guidance for living a God-honouring life. On the whole, the Bible serves as great food for daily encouragement and guidance.

You will also read a lot about the Father, the Son, and of the Holy Spirit. The Holy Spirit is the One who will play an important part in your growth and development. He will take whatever you read in the Bible and help you understand it. He will highlight certain portions to you on a daily basis and through these portions He will bring guidance, direction, encouragement and hope to you.

God desires to be in a living relationship with you!

God wants to have a relationship with you and He desires to speak to you. He speaks to us through the Bible and through the Holy Spirit, who will be speaking inside of us, through others bringing us a message from Him, or whilst we are praying. Through this course you will learn to know the Voice of God. We grow in our faith, and are fed through spending time in reading the Bible, by praying and by being discipled. For now, prayer is you talking to God about anything and everything, privately. This course will help you to develop each one of these areas.

If you have not committed your life to Christ, I pray that the Holy Spirit will bring you to that point of realizing your need for God. I pray that God will place one of His children in your life to show His love and care for you.

John 3:16 (NKJV)
"*16 For God so loved the world that He gave His only begotten Son,
that whoever believes in Him should not perish but have
everlasting life.*

Jesus loves you and desires a deep and meaningful relationship with you. He wants you to be part of His Family. You were born for a purpose. I pray that you will enjoy this journey into a relationship with the Living God and in finding your purpose in life.

Discipleship Foundations Series outline:

STEP ONE - SALVATION

The first phase of discipleship deals with the germination of our seed of faith. This phase deals with the essentials, or elementary applications of putting our faith in Jesus Christ as Lord. We will explore the elementary principles, as described in Hebrews chapter 6 verses 1 and 2.

STEP TWO – ESTABLISHING ROOTS, VALUES AND DISCIPLINES

The second phase deals with establishing **roots** from which our faith will grow and mature. Instilling the Values of the Kingdom of God, develops our spiritual roots. We also develop spiritual disciplines, to keep and maintain these values in our lives.

STEP THREE – DEVELOPING GIFTS AND SKILLS

The third phase of Discipleship deals with discovering and developing our spiritual gifts. It is the time when we learn, and develop, ministry skills to fulfill our calling in service of the Lord. These will help us to bring forth healthy fruit, take our stand against the evil one, and responsibly shepherd those whom we lead to faith in Jesus Christ.

STEP FOUR - FRUITFULNESS

The fourth phase of Discipleship deals with us, putting into practice what we've learnt, consistently living a life of love, and shepherding those entrusted to our care.

STEP FIVE - MULTIPLICATION

The fifth phase of Discipleship deals with our Disciples multiplying themselves through their Disciples, by helping and guiding them to consistently put into practice what they've learnt, and to help their Disciples to do the same. We model it to them by living a life of love, that remains worth following, and shepherding them into their purpose.

Discipleship is a journey.

This journey is made up of a few phases. It is called a Discipleship journey from which you will benefit most if you follow them through systematically from Step One to Step Five. This course will take you at least One Year to complete, however, as with living trees, it takes a lifetime to grow into a mighty tree. By daily drawing sap through our spiritual roots, being firmly grounded in the Word, prayer and in Fellowship, we will grow slowly and steadily.

When we look a little closer at each one of these five phases, we liken it to the Parable of the Sower where we see the first four phases of growth and development outlined, but with an emphasis on the condition of our hearts in receiving the Word of God.

This Discipleship Foundation Series is designed for people who desire to, not just receive the Word with gladness, but to receive it and allow it to grow until a multiplied harvest is reaped. I pray, that through the duration of this discipleship course, you will commit your life to Christ, or, as you go through the sessions, affirm your decision to accept Jesus as the Lord and Saviour of your soul. My prayer for you is that the Word of God, sown through this course, will not be snatched by Satan, but will germinate, take root and grow into maturity, to fruitfulness, and finally to a multiplied life.

> Luke 8:20 (NKJV) "*20 But these are the ones sown on good ground, those who hear the word, accept it, and bear fruit: some thirtyfold, some sixty, and some a hundred.*"

I pray that you will be that person in whose heart the seed of the Word of God will take root, endure through tribulations and persecutions, and persevere through the deceitful, worldly temptations, until you finally become fruitful with souls and see them multiply greatly.

Salvation Overview Diagram

Step One – Salvation

"Jesus said...unless one is born again, he can not see the Kingdom of God." John 3:3 NKJV

Step One explores the essentials, to allow the incorruptible Seed of God's Word, to take root in our lives, so that we can believe, and be saved. During this first Step of our Discipleship Foundations Series, we will look at these six elementary principles, which form the Foundation upon which we will build our journey in Christ.

Six Foundational Principles

The writer to the Hebrews outlines the six foundational principles in following Christ.

> Hebrews 6:1-2 (NKJV) "*1 Therefore, leaving the discussion of **the elementary principles of Christ,** let us go on to perfection, not laying again **the foundation** of repentance **from dead works** and of **faith toward God**, 2 of **the doctrine of baptisms**, of **laying on of hands**, of **resurrection of the dead**, and of **eternal judgment**.*"

Within these two verses we find the **elementary principles of life in Christ**, the only foundation upon which a living relationship with Jesus Christ is possible. They are:

1. Repentance from dead works,
2. Faith towards God,
3. Baptisms,
4. Laying on of Hands,
5. Resurrection of the dead, and
6. Eternal judgment.

If we build our faith upon these elementary principles, and add to them spiritual disciplines, and the development of good and sound spiritual roots, it will set us up for tremendous growth, and we will see the Seed of God produce in us fruitfulness.

The Departure Point.

The departure point in following Christ, is to understand sin, and its impact on our wellbeing. We need an understanding of our need for a Saviour, through Christ's Redemptive provision, by dying on the cross of Calvary for our sins. We can be saved, and redeemed from our sins, by acknowledging our sinfulness, and by confession and repentance of our sins, and receiving His forgiveness. The goal of this process is that we might be restored in our relationship with our Heavenly Father, His Son and with the Holy Spirit.

How can we be "Saved?"

To be "***SAVED***" requires two worlds to meet: **the Divine** and **Human worlds**. To be "***SAVED***" requires mankind to respond affirmatively to the divine work of God; through the Redemptive work of Christ on the Cross, by paying for our sins, and through the Holy Spirit's conviction inside of us.

To be "***SAVED***" is the process of being "***Born Again,***" or to put it in other words, it is to become a "***Child of God.***"

To be "Saved" is to be "Converted."

From a human perspective, this process of becoming a Child of God is called: "***Conversion,***" and is the voluntary change in the mind of a sinner, on one the one hand, ***from sin***, and on the other hand, ***to Christ***. This human perspective is not the result of human initiation, but a mere response to the work of the Holy Spirit inside of us. The ***turning from our sin is called Repentance***, and the ***turning to Christ is called Faith***.

To be "Saved" is to be "Regenerated."

From a Godly perspective, this process is called "***Regeneration,***" and is the act of God whereby God makes us new creations, creates in us a new heart and puts a new spirit within us. This act of God is further extended by God removing our sin, the wall of separation removed between Him and us, and Him making us holy and pure as He is, declaring us righteous. This is when we are "**born again.**"

It is a simultaneous process!

Even though this process of "***being saved***" is explained in different parts, this "***Union with Christ,***" through regeneration and conversion, is a simultaneous process. One describes the process from a Divine side and the other from a human side.

The first two parts that we will explore together deal specifically with our part in 'Conversion," and then in the third part we find conclusion in the "God" part of us being "Regenerated." Part 1 - Repentance from dead works, describes the "our" part in turning away from sin, and Part 2 - Faith towards God describes the "our" part in turning towards God in faith.

So, let's take our first step into this exciting Discipleship journey by looking at Part 1, of 6, in Step One – Salvation.

PART I

REPENTANCE FROM DEAD WORK

The departure point, in following Christ, should be "*repentance*" from dead works. Many think that they can come closer to God by doing good works, but there is only one way to come close to God and that is through Faith in Jesus Christ.

Repentance marks "our part" in Salvation.

The message Jesus preached in His day, to bring people to faith, was primarily a message, linking up with that of His predecessor John the Baptist, of Repentance. Repentance marks "**our part**" in responding to the work of the Holy Spirit inside of us.

Repentance might seem like a big word for someone who is exploring faith in Jesus. So, allow me to take you on a journey to understanding the value of this first part towards becoming a Child of God.

The Beginning.

From the beginning God had a good plan for mankind. Man was created by God.

Genesis 1:27 (NKJV) "*27 So **God created man in His own image; in the image of God He created him**; male and female He created them.*"

John 4:24 (NKJV) "*24 **God is Spirit**, and those who worship Him must worship in spirit and truth.*"

1 Thessalonians 5:23 (NKJV) "*23 Now may the God of peace Himself sanctify you completely; and **may your whole spirit, soul, and body** be preserved blameless at the coming of our Lord Jesus Christ.*"

We were created in the image of God.

From the beginning God intended for us **to be like Him** and **to live in fellowship with Him**. We know from the Bible that God is Spirit, and we, therefor, are spiritual beings. We know this from this Scripture, and many others, that we are spiritual beings. We are spirit beings who have a soul and live in a physical body.

Scofield once said: "*Because man is a "**spirit**," he is capable of God-consciousness, and of communion with God; because he is a "**soul**," he has self-consciousness; because he is a "**body**," he has, through his sense, world-consciousness.*"

Inside of each one of us there is this God-consciousness. There is this void or spiritually deadness which can only be filled or resolved when we are "Born again." We all have a "soul," which consists of our mind, intellect and emotion, and it is here that we make choices, some for better and some for worse. Adam and Eve made a choice to disobey God and hence sin and death came to all of us.

The Fall of Adam and Eve had devastating effects for mankind.

Adam and Eve sinned. They made a choice to disobey God in the Garden of Eden and through their actions of disobedience **sin came** and **death came**, and through their disobedience separation from the Presence of God came.

> 1 Corinthians 15:21-22 (NKJV) "*21 For since **by man came death, by Man also came the resurrection of the dead**. 22 For as **in Adam all die**, even **so in Christ all shall be made alive**.*"

> Romans 5:12 (NKJV) "*12 Therefore, just as **through one man sin entered the world, and death through sin, and thus death spread to all men, because all sinned**.*"

> Ephesians 2:1 (NKJV) "*1 And **you He made alive, who were dead in trespasses and sins**,*"

> Ephesians 2:4-5 (NKJV) "*4 But God, who is rich in mercy, because of His great love with which He loved us, 5 **even when we were dead in trespasses, made us alive together with Christ** (by grace you have been saved),*"

Sin came into the world and all of us have been affected by it. This is sometimes called imputed sin into mankind. **Through sin we became spiritually dead**. Through sin we got separated from God. It is only with Jesus in our lives that we come alive again.

Sin separates us from God.

Ever since the beginning, when Adam and Eve sinned in the Garden of Eden, through their disobedience, sin was passed down through mankind from generation to generation. In fact, the Bible says that: "***All have sinned and fall short of the Glory of God***."

> Isaiah 59:2-3 (NKJV) "*2 But **your iniquities have separated you from your God**; And **your sins have hidden His face from you, So that He will not hear**. 3 For your hands are defiled with blood, And your fingers with iniquity; Your

lips have spoken lies, Your tongue has muttered perversity."

Romans 5:12 (NKJV) "*12 Therefore, just as **through one man sin entered the world**, and **death through sin**, and thus death spread to all men, **because all sinned**.*"

Romans 3:10 (KJV) "*[10] As it is written, **There is none righteous, no, not one**:*"

All of us sinned.

All of us sinned and are in need of forgiveness of our sins. Sin has a devastating effect on our lives. If we fail to repent of our sins then they leave us spiritual dead. Sin separates us from God. Sin blinds us.

2 Corinthians 4:3-4 (NKJV) "*3 But even **if our gospel is veiled, it is veiled to those who are perishing**, 4 **whose minds the god of this age has blinded, who do not believe**, lest the light of the gospel of the glory of Christ, who is the image of God, should shine on them.*"

Isaiah 53:6 (NKJV) "*6 **All we** like sheep **have gone astray; We have turned, every one, to his own way**; And the Lord has laid on Him the iniquity of us all.*"

Romans 3:23 (NIV) "²³ for ***all have sinned*** and fall short of the glory of God,"

What will redeem us from sin?

The only redeeming price for sin is the <u>blood</u> of Jesus. In the Old Testament people sacrificed animals to pay for the redemption of their sins. Jesus Christ came and paid the price for our sins so that we, through putting our faith in Him, will receive forgiveness of our sins.

1 Peter 1:18-19 (NKJV) "*18 knowing that you were not redeemed with corruptible things*, like silver or gold, from your aimless conduct received by tradition from your fathers, 19 **but with the precious blood of Christ, as of a lamb without blemish and without spot.**"

We need a Saviour!

Christ is our <u>Saviour</u>. Only He can take our sins away. Only He made a way to take away our sins and to bring us into a restored relationship with the Father.

Luke 2:11 (NKJV) "*11 For there is born to you this day in the city of David **a Saviour, who is Christ the Lord.**"

Matthew 1:21 (NKJV) "*21 And she will bring forth a Son, and you shall call His name **Jesus**, for **He will save His people from their sins.**"

Acts 5:31 (NKJV) "*31 Him God has exalted to His right hand to be Prince and Saviour, **to give repentance to Israel and forgiveness of sins.**"

Romans 5:8 (NKJV)
"***8 But God demonstrates His own love toward us**, in that while we were still sinners, Christ died for us.*"

Christ died for <u>our</u> sins.

Christ showed His love towards us **by dying on our behalf, to pay for the penalty of our sin** and **to deliver us from the power and stronghold of sin.** He became the Lamb that was slain for the redemption of our souls. He gave His live that we, who deserved to die for our sins, might live.

. . .

Unless we make a heartfelt decision to turn away from our sins with true repentance, no enduring change is possible. There are a number of essential, non-negotiable landmarks for this discipleship journey to be successful, and this is most certainly one of them. Only start this discipleship journey if you want to turn from your sins and follow Christ.

On the day of Pentecost, Peter stood up and boldly preached a message, calling everyone to "**repent, be baptised and to wait for the gift of the Holy Spirit.**"

> Acts 2:37-38 (NKJV) "*37 Now when they heard this, they were cut to the heart, and said to Peter and the rest of the apostles, "**Men and brethren, what shall we do?**" 38 Then Peter said to them, "**Repent, and let every one of you be baptized** in the name of Jesus Christ for the remission of sins; **and you shall receive the gift of the Holy Spirit.**"*

What does it mean to "Repent?"

Repentance means that you make a roundabout turn in your <u>thoughts</u> and <u>actions</u>. **Repentance is to change your mind and actions, to conform to the Will and purpose of God.**

Defining: Repentance

The Vines Greek Dictionary describes the Greek word "metanoea" translated "Repentance" as:

"metanoea (μετανοέω - G3340), lit., "*to perceive afterwards*" (meta, "after," implying "*change*"; and, noea, "*to perceive*"; nous, "*the mind, the seat of moral reflection*"."

> Acts 2:38 (AMP) "*[38] And Peter answered them, **Repent (change your views and purpose to accept the will of God in your inner selves instead of rejecting it)** and be baptized, every one of you, in the name of Jesus Christ for the forgiveness of and release from your sins; and you shall receive the gift of the Holy Spirit.*"

What we see here is that:

*"**Repentance is a place we come to in our lives where we look at our lives with <u>sorrow</u>, reflect over our actions with <u>remorse</u>, and then turn <u>away</u> from our sins, <u>change</u> our course, our views and <u>accept</u> the Will of God, over ours.**"*

The way we give expression to this "change of heart and mind" is that we express true sorrow for our actions, behaviour and sins, and then confess our sins.

2 Corinthians 7:9-11 (NKJV) "*9 Now I rejoice, not that you were made sorry, but that **your sorrow led to repentance.** For you were made sorry in a godly manner, that you might suffer loss from us in nothing. 10 **For godly sorrow produces repentance leading to salvation,** not to be regretted; but the sorrow of the world produces death. 11 **For observe this very thing, that you sorrowed in a godly manner:** What **diligence** it produced in you, what **clearing** of yourselves, what **indignation,** what **fear,** what **vehement desire,** what **zeal,** what **vindication!** In all things you proved yourselves to be clear in this matter.*"

Hence we could say that repentance means more than being sorry for what has been done, although *<u>sorrow</u> always accompanies true repentance. Repentance also means that we stop sinning*, deliberately. *True sorrow will lead to repentance and that will lead you to salvation.*

Luke 19:8-10 (NKJV) "8 Then Zacchaeus stood and said to the Lord, "***Look, Lord, I give half of my goods to the poor***; and if ***I have taken anything from anyone by false accusation, I restore fourfold.***" 9 And Jesus said to him, "***Today salvation has come to this house***, because he also is a son of Abraham; 10 for the Son of Man has come to seek and to save that which was lost."

Repentance requires a change in our conduct, and this should be visible in us making right what we have done wrong. For Zacchaeus it was restoring what he took under false testimony. *The fruit of repentance is a changed life.*

How do we "Repent"?

- **We Repent when we accept the Holy Spirit's conviction inside of us.**

The Bible says that the Holy Spirit is now that active agent working inside of us to help us come to a place of repentance. **The Holy Spirit convicts us of sin**.

> John 16:8-11 (NKJV) "*8 And when He (Holy Spirit) has come, **He will convict the world of sin**, and of righteousness, and of judgment: 9 **of sin, because they do not believe in Me**; 10 of righteousness, because I go to My Father and you see Me no more; 11 of judgment, because the ruler of this world is judged.*"

I pray that you too will find the conviction of the Holy Spirit in your heart today to turn from your past life, from your sins, and choose to live in agreement with the will of God.

- **We come to repentance when we listen to God and stop hardening our hearts.**

> Hebrews 4:7 (NKJV) "*Today, if you will hear His voice, Do not harden your hearts.*"

Repentance requires for us to respond affirmatively to the conviction that the Holy Spirit is bringing inside of us. We need to say: "*Yes Lord, I have sinned. I have been doing things my way and not Your way.*" Take time to allow this conviction to work its way through in you. Confess your sins!

- **We come to repentance when we make confession of our sins.**

We have this assurance that when we confess our sins that He will forgive us our sins and cleanse us.

1 John 1:9 (NKJV) "*9 If we confess our sins, He is faithful and just to forgive us our sins and to cleanse us from all unrighteousness.*"

I encourage you to go to a quiet place and write down all the sins, areas where you might have sinned or did things your way and not God's way, and then make confession of these things, repent of them, and ask for God's Forgiveness. The thoroughness with which you do this will serve you well and produce tremendous changes in you. You might actually feel light, as if a weight came off your shoulders. The relief will be tangible. Sin weighs us down.

If you sense that God is bringing you to the point of repentance, don't resist His work in you. Even if you feel overcome by emotion and remorse over the things you've done and the life you lived, don't let it disturb or upset you, this is the work of the Holy Spirit. In most instances this sorrow brings forth repentance that truly bring us to a place of full surrender to the Lordship of Jesus.

If you have truly confessed your sins and repented of them, then thank God for His Forgiveness. The next part is extremely important! The next part runs **concurrently** with the first and that is to put your faith in Jesus as your Saviour.

ASSIMILATION SHEET
REPENTANCE OF DEAD WORKS

1. Which Scripture had the greatest impact on your decision today? _____

   Why?_____

   _____

   _____

2. How do you "Repent"? _____

   _____

   _____

   _____

3. How do you know that someone has truly 'Repented"? _____

   _____

   _____

   _____

4. Write out Acts 2:38 _____

   _____

   _____

   _____

5. How would you describe the importance of the following in Repentance:

Sorrow - _____

_____

_____

Restitution - _____

_____

_____

Confession - _____

_____

_____

PRAYER

I want to pray for you.

"Heavenly Father, I thank you that you died on the cross for our sins, and that by us repenting of them, that you offer us forgiveness. This is incredible Grace and Love. Thank you for saving my new brother or sister. Thank you that we could be part of Your Family. Amen"

PART II

FAITH IN GOD

The second part of being born again is to "***put your faith in God***." Jesus, spoke to Nicodemus and explained to him that he needed to be '***Born again***' to enter into the Kingdom of God. Unless a person ***repents***, places their ***faith in God***, and ***accepts Christ as their Lord*** and Saviour, no conversion or regeneration can take place.

Christ describes this conversion experience as being "***born again.***" Being "***Born Again***" marks the beginning of our discipleship journey. This is not possible until we've accepted Christ's redemptive work on the cross, and bowed to His Lordship in our lives.

> John 3:3-5 (NKJV) "3 Jesus answered and said to him, "Most assuredly, I say to you, **unless one is born again, he cannot see the kingdom of God.**" 4 Nicodemus said to Him, "How can a man be born when he is old? Can he enter a second time into his mother's womb and be born?" 5 Jesus answered, "Most assuredly, I say to you, **unless one is born of water and the Spirit, he cannot enter the kingdom of God.**"

To be **'Born again**" requires of us to "**repent**" of our sins, <u>yield</u> to the conviction of the Holy Spirit inside of us, AND, ***put our faith in Jesus Christ***.

People place their faith in many things. They place their faith in themselves (**humanism,**) in things like possessions (**materialism,**) traditions - especially those of their forefathers (**traditionalism,**) religion (**pharisaism,**) and many other things or people, except in God. They think that their security and stability is reliant on these things, other than on God. **For true conversion and regeneration to take place in our lives we need to also bow our knees to His Lordship, Jesus Christ, and make Him the Lord of our lives.** We need to put our faith in Him.

How do I put my faith in Jesus Christ?

The english language have two words to describe the same principle: a noun, FAITH; and a verb, TO BELIEVE.

The definition for "Faith" is:

> "***Faith is confidence or trust in** <u>**a person**</u> **or thing; or the observance of an obligation from** <u>**loyalty**</u>**; or fidelity to a** <u>**person**</u>**, promise, engagement. The word "faith" may also refer to a particular system of religious belief, in which faith may equate to confidence based on some perceived degree of warrant*.**"

We can conclude, that to have faith, is to believe.

What do we believe, to be true about Jesus Christ, so that we could have faith in Him?

- **We believe that Jesus is the <u>Son</u> of God.**

The first place we need to look at, in putting our faith in God, is **<u>who</u>** we put our faith in. Jesus is at the centre of this journey.

Jesus is a man who lived 2000 years ago.

Jesus is a man who lived around 2000 years ago in what is known today as Israel. Many Roman historians wrote about Him and His life during His earthly time with us. Some of these are Tacitus & Suetonius. He is not some mystical figure who might have lived. He was a real person with feelings, emotions and experience temptations and challenges just like us.

A Jewish historian, Josephus, also wrote about the impact of His life and ministry whilst being here on earth. The account from these historians are accepted as valid since there was a number of consistent copies found, which in one way validates the Bible as a reputable source of information. The consistency in the copies of manuscripts validates their content.

According to Nicky Gumble, in a comparative table, the validity and repute of New Testament writings and reports can, and should, therefor be upheld to substantiate the Person of Jesus Christ. So, I want to use these writings and reporting accounts, from various writers, to tell you about Jesus and what is so incredible that He did for us, that we should put our faith in Him.

Jesus is the <u>Son</u> of God.

The Apostle Matthew records an appearance of an Angel to Joseph, when he learnt that his fiancé was pregnant and explored options to privately leave her, where the Angel made it abundantly clear that she became pregnant by the Holy Spirit, something too wonderful for us to comprehend, and confirmed to him that she was bearing "Immanuel - meaning: God with us."

Matthew 1:23 (NKJV) "23 "Behold, *the virgin shall be with child*, and bear a Son, and they shall call His name *Immanuel*," which is translated, "*God with us*.""

The Apostle Matthew gives us a few accounts where they heard a voice from Heaven saying that Jesus was God's Son. The first was when

He was baptised, and the second was when He was on the Mountain with Peter, John

> Matthew 3:17 (NKJV) "17 And suddenly a voice came from heaven, saying, "**This is My beloved Son**, in whom I am well pleased.""

Jesus once asked His Disciples who people say that He was. The Apostle Peter stated, and it is recorded in Matthew, that He is "the Christ, the Son of the Living God."

> Matthew 16:15-16 (NKJV) "15 He said to them, "But who do you say that I am?"16 Simon Peter answered and said, "You are the Christ, **the Son** of the living God.""

On one occasion Jesus went up on a mountain with Peter, James and John and a bright cloud covered them, and they saw Jesus transfigured, alongside Moses and Elijah. On this occasion they also **heard a voice from heaven** affirming that Jesus was God's Son.

> Matthew 17:5(NKJV) "5 While he was still speaking, behold, a bright cloud overshadowed them; and suddenly a voice came out of the cloud, saying, "*This is My beloved Son, in whom I am well pleased. Hear Him!*""

When people asked Jesus whether He was the Son of God, He affirmed it. Now this would be blasphemy if He made such a claim and wasn't.

> Matthew 26:63-64 (NKJV) "63 But Jesus kept silent. And the high priest answered and said to Him, "I put You under oath by the living God: *Tell us if You are the Christ, the Son of God!*" 64 Jesus said to him, "*It is as you said.* Nevertheless, I say to you, hereafter you will see the Son of Man sitting at the right hand of the Power, and coming on the clouds of heaven.""

We can conclude that He is the "**Son of God**."

- **We believe that He <u>died</u> on the Cross of Calvary for our sins.**

What did Jesus do on earth?

Throughout the New Testament, especially the first few that are called the Gospels, we learn that Jesus came to "***take away the sins of mankind.***" His earthly assignment was declared from the beginning.

> Matthew 1:21 (NKJV) "21 And she will bring forth a Son, and you shall ***call His name Jesus***, for ***He will save His people from their sins.***""

The Apostle John reports that God sent His Son to die for us.

> John 3:16 (NKJV) "16 ***For God so loved the world that He gave His only begotten Son***, that whoever believes in Him should **<u>not perish</u>** but have everlasting life."

Why is sin such a big problem?

Sin separates us from God.

As we learnt in the previous session, Sin is an inherent problem and one that keeps us separated from God.

> Isaiah 59:2-3 (NKJV) "2 But ***your iniquities have <u>separated</u> you from your God***; And ***your <u>sins</u> have hidden His face from you***, So that He will not hear. 3 For your hands are defiled with blood, And your fingers with iniquity; Your lips have spoken lies, Your tongue has muttered perversity. Sin have polluted all of us. Sin is inside of us."

Sin is inside of us.

The Gospel according to mark tells us that this **sin is inside of us**.

> Mark 7:21-23 (NKJV) "21 For *from within, out of the heart of men, proceed evil* thoughts, adulteries, fornications, murders, 22 thefts, covetousness, wickedness, deceit, lewdness, an evil eye, blasphemy, pride, foolishness. 23 *All these evil things come from within and defile a man.*""

Christ died for our sins.

Christ died for our sins, and through His death and the price He paid, freed us from the power that sin had over us.

> 1 Peter 2:24 (NKJV) "24 who *Himself bore our sins in His own body on the tree*, that we, having died to sins, might live for righteousness—by whose stripes you were healed."

> Galatians 3:13 (NKJV) "13 *Christ has redeemed us from the curse of the law, having become a curse for us* (for it is written, "Cursed is everyone who hangs on a tree"),"

Only Christ can break the stronghold of this sin by paying the price for the sin, and redeeming us. Now we can be reconciled with the Father through this sacrificial show of love towards us by dying on a cross.

> 2 Corinthians 5:21 (NKJV) "21 For *He made Him who knew no sin to be sin for us*, that we might become the righteousness of God in Him."

> 2 Corinthians 5:18 (NKJV) "18 Now all things are of God, *who has reconciled us to Himself through Jesus Christ*, and has given us the ministry of reconciliation,"

Only One person can free you from your sins. His Name is Jesus. Put your faith in Him. He paid the price with His own life and he shed His blood for the forgiveness of your sins.

- **We believe that He <u>rose</u> from the dead and is <u>alive</u> and seated on the <u>right</u> hand of God the Father.**

Before Jesus died on the cross He declared to His Disciples that He would rise from the dead. This was an amazing message, and one profoundly confronting to a society that lived as if this life is all that there is. He spoke on the resurrection, and eternal life. Faith in Jesus is about believing in eternal life, but that life is only secure because Jesus rose from the dead.

> Romans 14:9 (NKJV) "9 For to this end ***Christ died and rose and lived again***, that He might be Lord of both the dead and the living."

Of course there are a few theories around which try to discount this claim of the resurrection of Jesus Christ from the dead, however, may I present to you what we believe.

Did He die?

Was He not just translated or transfigured like Enoch and Elijah. No, He suffered a dreadful and painful death on the cross on Calvary. He died and rose from the dead, in full knowledge of many, as recorded in some historical writings of Josephus:

> "(Josephus: The Writings of Flavius Josephus) *Now, there was about this time Jesus, a wise man, if it be lawful to call him a man, for he was a doer of wonderful works--a teacher of such men as receive the truth with pleasure. He drew over to him both many of the Jews, and many of the Gentiles. He was [THE] Christ; (64) and when **Pilate**, at the suggestion of the principal men amongst us, had **condemned him to the cross**, those that loved him at the first did not forsake him, for*

he appeared to them alive again the third day, as the divine prophets had foretold these and ten thousand other wonderful things concerning him; and the tribe of Christians, so named from him, are not extinct at this day."

We can most certainly conclude that He died. Let's look at a few Scriptures together.

Firstly, the Apostle John accounts that one of **the soldiers pierced _a spear_ into Jesus' side** and **he saw water and blood coming out**, indicating that He was dead already.

> John 19:34-35 (NKJV) "34 But one of **the soldiers pierced His side with a spear, and immediately blood and water came out**. 35 And **he who has seen has testified, and his testimony is true; and he knows that he is telling the truth, so that you may believe**."

We can be sure that the Roman soldiers would have ensured that Christ died on the cross to which He was sentenced. He definitely died. They wanted this "revolutionary" to get out of the way, but more than their desire to see Him dead, was the desire of the "Religious Establishment", namely the chief priests, the Council of Elders, and the teachers of the law, who would have followed the procession to be sure that He dies on that cross.

Secondly, we have the account of ***Pilate sending soldiers to seal and secure the tomb***. After His death He was buried in a newly cut grave tomb. The chief priests and Pharisees not only wanted Christ to be dead, but they wanted to ensure that He remains in the grave. Once they witnessed that Christ died, they went to Pilate and requested that the Tomb be sealed

> Matthew 27:62-66 (NKJV) "62 On the next day, which followed the Day of Preparation, the chief priests and Pharisees gathered together to Pilate, 63 saying, "Sir, we remember, while He was still alive, how that deceiver said, 'After three days I will rise.' 64 Therefore command that the tomb be

made secure until the third day, lest His disciples come by night and steal Him away, and say to the people, 'He has risen from the dead.' So the last deception will be worse than the first." 65 *Pilate said* to them, "*You have a guard; go your way, make it as secure as you know how.*" 66 So *they went and made the tomb secure, sealing the stone and setting the guard.*"

We can be sure that both the Pharisees, chief priests and Roman guard did not want Jesus to rise from the dead. What an extraordinary step to keep a dead person in a grave. Yet, even after all their securing and guarding of the grave, Jesus rose from the grave.

Thirdly, we know that *when Mary came to the grave* on the first day of the week, *she found the stone rolled away and the tomb empty*.

Matthew 28:1-4 (NKJV) "1 Now after the Sabbath, as the first day of the week began to dawn, Mary Magdalene and the other Mary came to see the tomb. 2 And behold, *there was a great earthquake*; for *an angel of the Lord descended from heaven, and came and rolled back the stone from the door*, and sat on it. 3 His countenance was like lightning, and his clothing as white as snow. 4 And *the guards shook for fear of him, and became like dead men*."

Here, again, we see the presence of the Roman guards, but they were frightened by what happened, as an Angel of God came down to open the grave. The guards were shaken by what they observed. The Angel had this amazing message for them and the two Mary's:

Matthew 28:6 (NKJV) "6 *He is not here; for He is risen, as He said*. Come, see the place where the Lord lay."

Now, it could be argued that a few tired and exhausted soldiers had an hallucination, but that is not where the resurrection account ended.

Fourthly, we see that **Jesus appeared to many people on different occasions**.

Jesus then continued to appear to both the Mary's, Peter, the Disciples, to 500 people in another place, in fact, over a 6 week period he appeared over 10 times to different people in different places.

Then of course we have the personal experience of a living God living inside of us. Jesus rose from the dead despite the precautions of the Roman guard, despite the objection of the chief priests, and despite the surprise of the disciples themselves.

Put your faith in Jesus Christ, because He is alive and wants to be your Saviour. We serve the living God, who gives life to all who put their faith in Him.

- **We believe that forgiveness for our sins is found from the Lord Jesus Christ.**

The ability and continued willingness to forgive is one of the most valuable attributes to embrace in any person's life, yet who brings forgiveness to our lives, when we have sinned, to such an extent, that we experience true release of the guilt and condemnation? Only in Jesus Christ, do we find such forgiveness from sins. Putting our faith in Jesus, is believing that He forgives us of all our sins, and redeems us through His blood.

> Ephesians 1:7 (NIV) [7] *In him we have redemption through his blood, the forgiveness of sins*, in accordance with the riches of God's grace."

> Acts 13:38 (NIV) [38] "Therefore, my brothers, I want you to know that *through Jesus the forgiveness of sins is proclaimed to you*."

We believe that if we confess our sins then He will forgive us and remove our sins. This is such an amazing promise: that upon confession of our sins, that God will forgive us. Confession of sins requires us to be honest both with ourselves and with God.

- **We come to believe, when we place our trust in Christ, to be our Lord and Saviour.**

Believing is essential, but the essential I am talking about is trusting Him to be our Master.

Bobby Harrington and Josh Patrick, in their book "**The Disciple Maker's Handbook**" tell a story of **Charles Blondin**, a tightrope walker, who in the mid 1800's became the first man to walk across the Niagara Falls on a tightrope made of hemp. The story goes that he would have walked over once, in full sight of a crowd of about 100'000 onlookers. He did it a second time with a chair, on which he stood when he came to the middle of the walk. Those who saw him do it stood in amazement. He then went a third time and cooked an omelette when he came to the middle of the rope, and then went on to ask his helpers to lower him to give the omelette to a passenger on the "Maid of the Mist" (a boat taking tourists for a close-up trip to the falls below.) He went a fourth time with a wheelbarrow. The crowd stood amazed at what they saw. He then asked them: Do you believe that I can walk across the Niagara Falls on a tightrope again? The resounding response from the crowd was very affirming: "Yes, of course we believe you can." "Well then" he said: "who will get into the wheelbarrow and let me push him across?" No one stepped forward except one man, Harry Colcord, a man who worked with him before. He not just believed that he could, but trusted him enough to climb into the wheelbarrow to be pushed across the tightrope. They completed this crossing successful again. This is what putting your faith in God requires.

Many say that they belief in Jesus, but not all those who say they belief in Him are actually willing to trust Him enough with their lives. Believing in Jesus requires us to get into the wheelbarrow and trust Jesus with our whole lives. It is one of the greatest blessings to know that with Him in control of our lives, we are not just save, but our future is save and secure.

We have the beautiful example in Acts 16 when Paul and Silas was in prison. The Lord sent an earthquake and all the prisoners chains came off and all the prison doors were opened. The jailer got such a fright that he wanted to kill himself. The Apostles Paul and Silas stopped the Jailer from killing himself, and shared the Good News of Jesus with him. He and his household accepted Jesus into their lives. They believed and got baptised.

> Acts 16:30-31, 33b, 34c (NKJV) "30 And he brought them out and said, "Sirs, **what must I do to be saved?**" 31 So they said, "**Believe on the Lord Jesus Christ, and you will be saved**, you and your household." "33 ... And **immediately he and all his family were baptized**. 34...; and he rejoiced, **having believed in God** with all his household."

The Jailer asked the question that we are exploring right now: "*What must I do to be saved?*" The answer came immediately: **"Believe on the Lord Jesus Christ, and you will be saved."** That message is still the same today: **"Believe on the Lord Jesus Christ, and you will be saved."** I encourage you to believe on the Lord Jesus with all your heart and you too will be saved.

On another occasion Philip was called to go to a certain road, and that is where he saw and met an Ethiopian Eunuch to whom he shared the Word. The conclusion of their journey through the Scriptures was that Philip made an 'altar call.' He made sure that this person believed in the Lord Jesus. After confession of his faith in the Lord Jesus they stopped and he got baptised.

> Acts 8: 37 (NKJV) "37 Then Philip said, "**If you believe with all your heart, you may**." And he answered and said, "**I believe that Jesus Christ is the Son of God.**"

The same is true for us today: If we believe that Jesus is the Son of God, that he died for our sins, and that He will save and forgive us our sins, then we too can be saved. It is interesting that the Lord added to the church those who were saved.

As mentioned earlier: **"Believe on the Lord Jesus Christ, and you will be saved."** When we believe in Jesus, we put our faith in

Him. We believe it from our hearts and therefor confess it with our mouths. Putting our faith in God requires both the believing of the heart and the confession with the mouth. This is also what the Word of God teaches us in Romans 10 verse 9:

> Romans 10:9 (NKJV) "*9 that if you <u>confess</u> with your mouth the Lord Jesus and <u>believe</u> in your heart that God has raised Him from the dead, you will be <u>saved</u>.*"

> Hebrews 11:6 (NKJV) "*6 But without faith it is impossible to please Him, for he who comes to God must believe that He is, and that He is a rewarder of those who diligently seek Him.*"

Maybe you've never confessed with your mouth that Jesus Christ is your Lord. Take this opportunity to say to the Lord Jesus: "*Jesus Christ, I want you to be the Lord over my life. Jesus Christ, I believe in you.*"

ASSIMILATION SHEET

FAITH IN GOD

1. Complete the sentence: *To be "**Born again**" requires us to <u>repent</u> of our sins, <u>yield</u> to the conviction of the Holy Spirit inside of us, AND, put our <u>faith</u> in Jesus Christ.*

2. The definition for "Faith" is: "*Faith is confidence or trust in <u>a person</u> or thing; or the observance of an obligation from <u>loyalty</u>; or fidelity to <u>a person</u>, promise and engagement.*

3. Complete the sentence: *Jesus is the <u>Son</u> of God.*

4. Complete the sentence: We believe that He on the Cross of Calvary for our sins.

5. Complete the sentence. *We believe that He <u>rose</u> from the dead and is <u>alive</u> and seated on the <u>right</u> hand of God the Father.*

6. How do we know Christ died?

   1. *The Soldiers pierced Jesus' side with a spear.*
   2. *Blood and water came from His side.*

3. *Pilate sealed the tomb, and placed guards at the Tomb for three days.*

7. How do we know that Christ rose from the dead?

   1. Mary found that the stone was rolled away, and that the tomb was empty.
   2. The Soldiers saw an Angel come down and roll away the stone.
   3. Jesus appeared to 500 people, to the twelve disciples and to the Emmaus disciples.

8. Complete the sentence: We believe that forgiveness for our sins is found only in Jesus Christ.

9. Complete the sentence: We believe, when we place our trust in Jesus, to be our Lord and Saviour.

10. What must I do to be saved? Complete the sentence: **"believe** on the Lord Jesus Christ, and you will be saved."

11. Complete the sentence: "If you confess with your mouth the Lord Jesus and believe in your heart that God has raised Him from the dead, you will be saved."

12. There are two aspects to Salvation, a human perspective, and a Divine perspective.

HOW CAN I BE BORN AGAIN?

In concluding the first two parts of being saved, let us remember that it is a combination of God working in us and us responding to His Gracious interaction with us.

Let us take a moment and look at the most important part of being saved, of being "Born again." The most important part is the Divine part, the part that describes the incredible work of God in us.

The Two Parts of Salvation

1. The <u>divine</u> part in Salvation

God called us out of Darkness, into a relationship with His Son, Jesus Christ. This represents the God part, or Divine part, of this amazing work, of being "Born again". He calls us to repent of our sins, through the working of His Holy Spirit's conviction inside of us. His part is extended in that, upon our yielding and submission and asking Him to be our Lord, and for His Gracious Forgiveness, He makes us New Creations. He restores our lives. He forgives us; He purifies us and cleanses us, and makes us one of His own children. This Divine part is amazing. We are truly "born again."

2 Corinthians 5:17 (NKJV) "17 Therefore, *if anyone is in Christ, he is a new creation*; old things have passed away; behold, *all things have become new*."

This Scripture confirms to us that when we are "Born again," He makes everything brand new. He makes us new creations. He takes away our old pasts and give us a fresh start in life. There is this Old Testament Scripture that describes it by stating that God will give us a new heart and a new spirit. I pray that this will be your experience as well that God will create in you a new heart and restore a right spirit inside of you.

Ezekiel 36:26 (NKJV) "26 *I will give you a new heart and put a new spirit within you;* I will take the heart of stone out of your flesh and give you a heart of flesh."

May your heart of stone be taken out and may you receive a heart of flesh. This is all the Gracious work of God who makes everything new. The Word also tells us that, when we believe, that He justifies us.

Acts 13:39 (NKJV) "39 and by Him *everyone who believes is justified from all things* from which you could not be justified by the law of Moses."

He brings us into a new and close relationship with Himself. God always desired to be in an open relationship with us. Right from the garden of Eden times He desired to be in fellowship with His creation. Through Christ we can have a restored relationship with the Father, the Son and the Holy Spirit. Just open your heart, your life, to Him and let Him come in. This takes me to the human part of salvation.

Revelation 3:20 (NKJV) "20 Behold, I stand at the door and knock. *If anyone hears My voice* and *opens the door, I will come in to him and dine with him, and he with Me*."

2. The **Human** part in Salvation.

The Human part of this work of being "Born Again" is when we open our hearts to the messages brought to us through His Children. Our part is when we deeply consider our lives and actions, in the light of His internal conviction and the Words presented to us, and with remorse over our failure to acknowledge Him and His Graciousness extended to us, confess our sins, ask for His forgiveness, and ask Him to come and be the Lord of our lives.

The Bible tells us that this conversion experience of being Borg again, happens when we heed to His call to come out of Darkness into a relationship with His Son.

> 1 Peter 2:9 (NKJV) "9 *But you are a chosen generation, a royal priesthood, a holy nation, His own special people, that you may proclaim the praises **of Him who called you out of darkness into His marvelous light**;*"

Christ is calling you out of Darkness. Follow His call into the Light of God.

> Colossians 1:13-14 (NIV) "*[13] For **he has rescued us from the dominion of darkness** and brought us into the kingdom of the Son he loves, [14] **in whom we have redemption, the forgiveness of sins**.*"

I have often seen people come under deep conviction of the Holy Spirit for their sins, repent of them, but they never put their faith in Jesus to be the Lord over their lives. For true transformation to take place in our lives we need to transition our faith from ourselves to having faith in God for our entire lives.

"For true transformation to take place in our lives we need to transition our faith from ourselves to having faith in Jesus for our entire lives." Dr. Hendrik J. Vorster

How do I become Born Again?

We become born again when we come into agreement with God about our lostness and our need of Him. We become born again when God, in His Gracious Love brings such conviction in our hearts to, have remorse over our sins, confess them and repent thereof. We are born again when He gives us rebirth by the Holy Spirit. We become born again when we confess our sins and ask for His forgiveness. We become born again when we transition our faith from ourselves to believing on the Lord Jesus Christ. We are born again when all of this come into alignment simultaneously.

Let us take a moment and revisit the aspects of being born again:

1. Repent of your <u>sins</u>.

I pray that Godly Sorrow will fill your heart today, and that this sorrow will bring you to true confession and repentance of your sins.

> 2 Corinthians 7:9-11 (NKJV) "*9 Now I rejoice, not that you were made sorry, but that **your sorrow led to repentance.** For you were made sorry in a godly manner, that you might suffer loss from us in nothing. 10 **For godly sorrow produces repentance leading to salvation,** not to be regretted; but the sorrow of the world produces death.*

2. Believe on the Lord Jesus Christ, and you will be saved.

I pray that faith, to believe, will rise in your heart. As you've listened to these Scriptures, I believe that the Holy Spirit activated faith in you to believe His Words. Respond to this work of the Holy Spirit inside of you and put your faith in Jesus Christ. Faith is a Gift of God.

> Romans 10:17 (NKJV) "*17 So then **faith comes by hearing, and hearing by the word of God.**"

Ephesians 2:8 (NKJV) "8 For by grace **you have been saved through faith**, and that not of yourselves; **it is the gift of God**,"

3. <u>Bow</u> your knees before Him and <u>confess</u> with your mouth that He is your Lord.

I pray that you will acknowledge Jesus Christ as your Lord and Saviour.

Romans 10:9 (NKJV) "**9 that if you confess with your mouth the Lord Jesus and believe in your heart that God has raised Him from the dead, you will be saved.**"

Acknowledge and confess with your mouth that you accept Jesus Christ as your Lord and Saviour, as you believe in your heart.

4. <u>Ask</u> Jesus to come into your life!

In speaking to the Church in Laodicea, the Holy Spirit called the Church to repentance with a promise that, if they did, and opened their hearts towards Him, that He would come in and make His Home with them. I pray that you too will open the door of your heart to the Lord Jesus and let Him come in and live with you.

Revelation 3:20 (NKJV) "20 Behold, I stand at the door and knock. **If anyone hears My voice and opens the door, I will come in to him and dine with him, and he with Me.**"

We have this amazing promise that when we receive Him in our lives, that we receive the right to become His children.

John 1:12-13 (NKJV) "12 **But as many as received Him, to them He gave the right to become children of God, to those who believe in His name**: 13 **who were born**, not of blood, nor of the will of the flesh, nor of the will of man, **but of God**."

Ask the Lord to come into your life. Ask Him to be your Lord and to save you from your sins. Ask Him to make you one of His Children. The godly sorrow you experience, connected with these simple prayers and actions is a work of God. Allow His work to continue in you to be born again.

When we respond to the work of the Holy Spirit inside of us, God does His part, and His part is an amazing part of us being "Born again."

Let's take a moment, and look at the miracle God performs, when we are "Born again."

1. You become a child of God.

> John 1:12-13 (NKJV) "*12 **But as many as received Him, to them He gave the right to become children of God, to those who believe in His name**: 13 **who were born**, not of blood, nor of the will of the flesh, nor of the will of man, **but of God**.*"

> 1 John 3:(NKJV) "*1 Behold what manner of love the Father has bestowed on us, **that we should be called children of God!**"*

2. You receive forgiveness of all your sins.

The Word of God says that, "God is Faithful and just," He will do His part and be faithful to fulfil His promise of forgiveness upon our confession of sin.

> 1 John 1:9 (NKJV) "*9 If we confess our sins, **He is faithful and just to forgive us our sins and to cleanse us from all unrighteousness**.*"

He not only will forgive us, He will also cleanse us from all unrighteousness. This is an amazing work of God. The Psalms gives us this promise that God will remove our transgressions from us, as far as the East is from the West. How awesome is that?

Psalm 103:12 (NKJV) *"12 As far as the East is from the West, So far has He removed our transgressions from us."*

Colossians 3:13-15 (NKJV) *"13 And you, being dead in your trespasses and the uncircumcision of your flesh,* **He has made alive together with Him, having forgiven you all trespasses,** *14* **having wiped out the handwriting of requirements that was against us,** *which was contrary to us. And* **He has taken it out of the way, having nailed it to the cross.** *15* **Having disarmed principalities and powers,** *He made a public spectacle of them,* **triumphing over them in it."**

3. The curse over your life is broken.

One of the many blessings we receive when we accept Christ, is that He breaks every curse over our lives. Many people live with a sense of being under a curse, and for many it is a very real reality of knowing that they and their family have been curse. Jesus Christ became a curse that you could be blessed. When you invite Jesus into your life, you invite the Blessing of God in, and He breaks every curse and spell over your life. The curse is broken.

Galatians 3:13-14 (NKJV) *"13* **Christ has redeemed us from the curse of the law,** *having become a curse for us (for it is written, "Cursed is everyone who hangs on a tree"), 14* **that the blessing of Abraham might come upon the Gentiles** *in Christ Jesus,* **that we might receive the promise of the Spirit through faith."**

4. You are taken out of darkness and brought into the light.

Colossians 1:13 (NKJV) *"13* **He has delivered us from the power of darkness** *and conveyed us into the kingdom of the Son of His love, 14* **in whom we have redemption through His blood, the forgiveness of sins."**

5. You become a New Creation.

2 Corinthians 5:17 (NKJV) "*17 Therefore, **if anyone is in Christ, he is a new creation**; old things have passed away; **behold, all things have become new**.*"

6. You come into spiritual union with Christ.

2 Corinthians 5:18 (NKJV) "*18 Now all things are of God, **who has reconciled us to Himself through Jesus Christ**, and has given us the ministry of reconciliation,*"

7. You are baptised into the Body of Christ.

1 Corinthians 12:13 (NKJV) "13 For by one Spirit we were all baptized into one body—whether Jews or Greeks, whether slaves or free—and have all been made to drink into one Spirit."

8. You become a part of the family of the Most High God.

2 Corinthians 6:18 (NIV) *18 "I will be a Father to you, and you will be my sons and daughters, says the Lord Almighty."*

We are all born into a family at natural birth. The same is true when we are "Born again." We are "Born" into the family of God. This new family needs to be embraced for us to benefit from the support everyone gives and receives. We are built up as we gather together. We show and receive love in this Family. Families normally do life together. One of the ways the family of God "do life together" is by making a commitment to be part of a Life group, and by committing to the meetings on weekends when the Believers gather together.

These just outline some of the many blessings bestowed upon us when we open our hearts and let Jesus become the Lord of our lives.

We become part of a Heavenly Family where God is our Father, Jesus our Brother and the Holy Spirit our constant Companion and Guide.

> Hebrews 3:7-12 (NIV) 7 So, as the Holy Spirit says: "Today, if you hear his voice, 8 do not harden your hearts as you did in the rebellion, during the time of testing in the desert, 9 where your fathers tested and tried me and for forty years saw what I did. 10 That is why I was angry with that generation, and I said, 'Their hearts are always going astray, and they have not known my ways.' 11 So I declared on oath in my anger, 'They shall never enter my rest.' " 12 See to it, brothers, that none of you has a sinful, unbelieving heart that turns away from the living God."

If you just followed these steps, and asked Jesus to come into your life, even if you did it previously but felt that you most certainly made that commitment today, then I encourage you to sign your Name below and date it accordingly.

Signature
    Date

PART III

BAPTISMS

Part 3, as outlined in the Scripture below, speaks of "**Baptisms**", in the plural. We have the **Baptism into the Body of Christ**, the **Baptism of Believers**, and **the Baptism of the Holy Spirit**. We have a number of Biblical examples to emphasise this **progression from Regeneration** (Baptism into the Body of Christ,) **to Baptism in water, to receiving the Baptism of the Holy Spirit**.

> Hebrews 6:1-2 (NKJV)
> "*1 Therefore, leaving the discussion of the elementary principles of Christ, let us go on to perfection, not laying again the foundation of repentance from dead works and of faith toward God, 2 of **the doctrine of baptisms**, of laying on of hands, of resurrection of the dead, and of eternal judgment.*"

Baptism into the Body of Christ.

In one sense we already discussed the first Baptism into the Body of Christ in our previous sessions, when we discussed about being "Born again." This is a work of God through the Holy Spirit at regeneration.

1 Corinthians 12:13 (NIV 1984)

13 For **we were all baptized by one Spirit into one body**—
whether Jews or Greeks, slave or free—and **we were all
given the one Spirit to drink**."

In this session we explore the next step, of baptism, as one of the
ordinances instituted by Christ for His followers to obey. Baptism
marks the next necessary step for those who turned their backs on
their past sins and turned towards Christ as Lord and who desire to
live their lives in union with Christ. Baptism is that step of obedience
signifying one's unification with the death and resurrection of Jesus
Christ.

In Biblical order we find, firstly, that when we accept Christ as
Lord, through conversion, we are baptised into the Body of Christ.
That regeneration process marks our immersion into the Body of
Christ, however, Baptism marks our installation into the Body of
Christ. It could be explained by comparing the election of a president
of a country. They might be elected, but only take office once they are
installed or sworn in. Baptism is that, "swearing in" ceremony. It is an
outward affirmation of change of mind and direction and of an inner
regeneration. This brings us to our discussion of the Baptism of
Believers.

The Baptism of Believers.

Jesus emphasized that **believers** should be baptised, as a necessary
step after believing.

Mark 16:16 (NIV)

[16] **Whoever believes and is baptized will be saved**, but
whoever does not believe will be condemned.

Method of Baptism.

The Biblical method of Baptism is by immersion. The Greek Word
for Baptise is the word "Baptismo" which means to **immerse**. In

Biblical times those who responded to the message of salvation, publicly went into deep running water and submersed themselves as a sign that they died with Christ and no longer live their old way of life but want to rise in a new life under Christ's ruler ship and reign. This method is still used in Christian Churches around the world today.

Who can be Baptised?

Believers can be Baptised, and in fact, should be baptised, for reasons to be explained next. Hence it is called the Baptism of Believers.

Baptism is for Believers.

Since the instruction is clear from Scripture that those who believe should be Baptised, we call it the "**Baptism of Believers.**"

Mark 16:15-16 (NKJV)

"15 And He said to them, "Go into all the world and preach the gospel to every creature. 16 **He who believes and is baptized will be saved**; but he who does not believe will be condemned.""

Matthew 28:19 (NKJV)

"19 Go therefore and **make disciples** of all the nations, **baptizing them in the name of the Father and of the Son and of the Holy Spirit**,"

What happens when we are baptised?

Through Baptism we <u>bury</u> our old selves and <u>rise</u> to a new life.

Baptism is an ordinance of the Church, not as some ritualistic man made requirement, but as one ordained by God. In fact there are two of these divinely ordained sacraments: baptism and communion (the Lord's Table.) These are called ordinances since they are ceremonies "*ordained*" by the Lord Jesus.

If we take the words of the Lord Jesus as a guideline, from His message to Nicodemus, then we see that entrance into the Kingdom of God is only possible through water and the spirit. Water signifies baptism and Spirit signifies the regenerative work of the Spirit at conversion, when we are "born again."

The "Born again" experience is truly a work of the Holy Spirit. It could be said that we are born of the spirit through the regenerative work of the Holy Spirit; however, being born of water depends on our obedience and willingness to be birthed out of the water, through baptism.

> John 3:5 (NIV)
> "[5] Jesus answered, "I tell you the truth, **no one can enter the kingdom of God unless he is born of water and the Spirit**."

The Church developed their requirement for entrance into the formal life of the Church upon this Scripture primarily: that as a sign of people's commitment to Christ, they go through the waters of baptism, and thus show their commitment and allegiance, and become part of the "Kingdom of God" - the Church.

Baptism is a sacrament.

Baptism is a ceremonial action we take to submerse ourselves in water, signifying our death to sin and the world, and burying our old selves, but then also, to signify, as we come out of the water, rising up to a new life with Christ through our reliance on His resurrection Power.

Let us take a moment and take a deeper look at the Baptism of Believers. Romans 6 summarises these two concepts beautifully.

> Romans 6:3-4 (NIV)
> "[3] Or don't you know that **all of us who were baptized into Christ Jesus were baptized into his death**? [4] *We were therefore buried with him through baptism into death* in order that, *just as Christ was raised from the dead* through the glory of the Father, *we too may live a new life*."

Galatians 3:27 (NIV)
"[27] for ***all of you who were baptized into Christ have clothed yourselves with Christ***."

Symbolism of Baptism explained:

Firstly, Into the water, speaks of <u>death</u> unto self.

Romans 6 verse 3 and 4 makes it clear that the first thing that happens in baptism is that we bury our old selves. We died to self when we asked Jesus to be the Lord of our lives. All we want to do now is live for Him. So, when you get baptised, you bury that old man, full of sin and death. As we go down into the water we are saying that Jesus died in our stead for our sins, and we also die to sin in our lives. We also declare through going into the water that we make a complete break with the past, and that is signified through death and burial. Baptism is that public declaration that I am done with my past life and I putting an end to it.

Secondly, Out of the water, speaks of <u>resurrection</u> to a new life, and <u>clothing</u> one self with Christ.

Romans 6 verse 4 goes on to explain that through baptism we also rise to a new life, just as Christ was raised from the dead to a new life. We rise to a new life when we come out of the water, but, as we come out of the water we also find ourselves born of water. There is of course another part to this baptism and that is that we clothe ourselves with Christ through baptism. This means that you take on yourself the life of Christ, to follow Him in humble obedience.

When will you be baptised?

Obedience is one of the hallmarks of believers! Ask the Pastor, Spiritual leader or person who led you to salvation to baptise you. Do so publicly as to declare to everyone that to made a firm commitment to follow Christ as the Lord of your life. When Philip preached the Word to the Ethiopian Eunuch, they came to a place where there was water, enough that it was said in verse 39 that: "***as they came out of the water...***" Baptism is complete when we do this publicly and by complete immersion.

The question is:

"***What hinders you from getting baptised today?***"

Acts 8:36-38 (NKJV)
"36 Now as they went down the road, they came to some water. And the eunuch said, "***See, here is water. What hinders me from being baptized?***" 37 Then Philip said, "***If you believe with all your heart, you may.***" And he answered and said, "***I believe that Jesus Christ is the Son of God.***" 38 So he commanded the chariot to stand still. And ***both Philip and the eunuch went down into the water, and he baptized him.***"

I pray that this will be you today! May God bless you as you follow Him in obedience through the waters of Baptism.

Baptism of the Holy Spirit.

Towards the end of Jesus' ministry He emphasized to His Disciples the importance of water baptism and the subsequent Baptism with the Holy Spirit.

Acts 1:5 (NIV)
*[5] For John baptized with water, but in a few days **you will be baptized with the Holy Spirit.***"

The Apostles preached the Gospel, and then immediately after people responded to the message, emphasized that these new believers should be baptised, and they received the Holy Spirit. The Apostle Peter presented this later Baptism as a promise from the Father.

Acts 2:37-38 (NKJV)

"37 Now when they heard this, they were cut to the heart, and said to Peter and the rest of the apostles, "Men and brethren, **what shall we do?**" 38 Then Peter said to them, **"Repent, and let every one of you be baptized** in the name of Jesus Christ for the remission of sins; **and you shall receive the gift of the Holy Spirit.**"

When Philip finished sharing the Gospel with people, he immediately baptised those who believed his message and placed their faith in Jesus Christ.

Acts 8:12 (NIV)

[12] But **when they believed** Philip **as he preached the good news** of the kingdom of God and the name of Jesus Christ, **they were baptized**, both men and women.

The Apostles were quite intentional in their pursuit of new believers. Once people accepted the Word of God, they immediately taught them about baptism as a means of sealing their new found faith with a public demonstration of solidarity with Christ, and then as an immediate follow up of their obedience to go through the waters of baptism, laid their hands on them to receive the Holy Spirit.

Acts 8:14-17 (NIV)

'[14] **When the apostles** in Jerusalem **heard that** Samaria **had accepted the word of God**, they sent Peter and John to them. [15] When they arrived, **they prayed for them that they might receive the Holy Spirit**, [16] because the Holy Spirit had not yet come upon any of them; **they had simply been baptized** into the name of the Lord Jesus. [17] **Then Peter and John placed their hands on them, and they received the Holy Spirit.**"

Acts 19:4-7 (NIV)

[4] Paul said, "John's baptism was a baptism of repentance. **He told the people to believe in the one coming after him, that is, in Jesus."** [5] On hearing this, **they were baptized into the name of the Lord Jesus.** [6] When **Paul placed his hands on them, the Holy Spirit came on them**, and they spoke in tongues and prophesied. [7] There were about twelve men in all.

In these few verses, among many New Testament examples, we find examples of an order of how the Apostles discipled. *We clearly see the progression from conversion/regeneration, to baptism in water, to baptism in the Holy Spirit.* These three basic initial elements of the Discipleship journey are essential starting blocks. We see that the disciples were intentional, to preach the Gospel, and then ensure that these new believers were Baptised, and then let them receive the Holy Spirit.

The third part of this session on Baptism is **equally important**, and that **involves the baptism with the Holy Spirit**. When the Apostles heard that Samaria received the Word of the Lord, they went over to pray for them that they might receive the Holy Spirit.

Acts 8:12 (NKJV)

"*12 But **when they believed Philip as he preached** the things concerning the kingdom of God and the name of Jesus Christ, **both men and women were baptized**.*"

Acts 8:14-17 (NIV)

'[14] **When the apostles** in Jerusalem **heard that** Samaria **had accepted the word of God**, they sent Peter and John to them. [15] When they arrived, **they prayed for them that they might receive the Holy Spirit**, [16] because the Holy Spirit had not yet come upon any of them; **they had simply been baptized** into the name of the Lord Jesus. [17] **Then Peter and John placed their hands on them, and they received the Holy Spirit**."

Why is this Baptism important for Believers?

The Baptism of the Holy Spirit is important since it was a Promise of something Jesus would bring.

Ever since the time John, the Baptist, started his ministry, he pointed to One that would come after him and would "*Baptise with the Holy Spirit.*" It seems from John's message that the real baptism they should seek is that of being baptised with the Holy Spirit.

> Matthew 3:11 (NKJV)
> "11 I indeed baptize you with water unto repentance, *but He who is coming after me is mightier than I*, whose sandals I am not worthy to carry. *He will baptize you with the Holy Spirit and fire.*"

We see that Jesus confirmed and continued to encourage His Disciples to wait for this Gift of the Holy Spirit in Acts 1 verses 4 to 5. What was this "*Promise of the Father?*" It was the "*Baptism with the Holy Spirit.*"

> Acts 1:4-5 (NKJV)
> "4 And being assembled together with them, He commanded them not to depart from Jerusalem, but to *wait for the Promise of the Father*, "which," He said, "you have heard from Me; 5 for John truly baptized with water, *but you shall be baptized with the Holy Spirit not many days from now.*"

We also see that Jesus promised that they would receive "*power*" when they would receive the Holy Spirit, and that they would be "*His witnesses.*"

> Acts 1:8 (NKJV) "8 But *you shall receive power when the Holy Spirit has come upon you*; and *you shall be witnesses* to Me in Jerusalem, and in all Judea and Samaria, and to the end of the earth."

We see in Acts chapter 2 verse 4 that they received the Baptism with the Holy Spirit.

Acts 2:4 (NKJV)
"4 And they were all filled with the Holy Spirit and began to speak with other tongues, as the Spirit gave them utterance."

Jesus spoke of this Gift of the Holy Spirit on a number of occasions during His ministry.

John 7:38-39 (NKJV)
"38 He who believes in Me, as the Scripture has said, out of his heart will flow rivers of living water." 39 But this He spoke concerning the Spirit, *whom those believing in Him would receive*; for the Holy Spirit was not yet given, because Jesus was not yet glorified."

The Baptism of the Holy Spirit is for Believers, and He would be an incredible help to the Believers.

John 14:26 (NKJV)
"26 But *the Helper, the Holy Spirit*, whom the Father will send in My name, *He will teach you all things, and bring to your remembrance all things that I said to you.*"

The Holy Spirit has a powerful ministry among us. His ministry is everything we need and desire in our lives for living successful godly lives. Once the Disciples, and all who were with them in the Upper room, were baptised in the Holy Spirit, they started to minister: Peter preached and we see 3000 came to the Lord that day. Since his message was clear, I believe that they baptised all 3000 and saw them receiving the Baptism with the Holy Spirit as well.

Let's look at Acts 2 verses 38 to 39:

Acts 2:38-39 (NKJV) 38 Then Peter said to them, "**Repent, and let every one of you be baptized in the name of Jesus Christ** for the remission of sins; and **you shall receive the gift of the Holy Spirit.** 39 For **the promise is to you and to your children, and to all who are afar off, as many as the Lord our God will call.**"

3000 people received Christ that day. The Apostles made sure that everyone who were "Born again" received the Holy Spirit.

Acts 8:14-17 (NKJV) 14 Now **when the apostles** who were at Jerusalem **heard that Samaria had received the word of God, they sent Peter and John to them,** 15 who, when they had come down, prayed for them that they might receive the Holy Spirit. 16 For as yet He had fallen upon none of them. **They had only been baptized in the name of the Lord Jesus.** 17 **Then they laid hands on them, and they received the Holy Spirit.**"

Some believe that we are Baptised with the Holy Spirit either when we are 'Born again" or when we go through the waters of Baptism, but this Scripture, and others, refute that thought process, since we see that the Apostles had to intervene and teach the new believers and then lay their hands on them to receive the Holy Spirit. This was also the practice of the Apostle Paul.

Acts 19:1-6 (NKJV)
"1 And it happened, while Apollos was at Corinth, that Paul, having passed through the upper regions, came to Ephesus. And finding some disciples 2 he said to them, "Did you receive the Holy Spirit when you believed?" So they said to him, "We have not so much as heard whether there is a Holy Spirit." 3 And he said to them, "Into what then were you baptized?" So they said, "Into John's baptism." 4 Then Paul said, "John indeed baptized with a baptism of repentance, saying to the people that they should believe on

Him who would come after him, that is, on Christ Jesus." 5 When they heard this, they were baptized in the name of the Lord Jesus. 6 And when Paul had laid hands on them, the Holy Spirit came upon them, and they spoke with tongues and prophesied."

Paul found some new believers in Ephesus. He wanted to make sure that they, as Believers, were baptised in the Holy Spirit, but soon found out that they were only baptised in John's baptism. Once He shared with them about the Baptism in the Name of Jesus, they were baptised and afterwards he laid his hands on them to receive the Baptism with the Holy Spirit. The Apostles seem to always make sure that people were Believers, baptised and filled with the Holy Spirit as a bare minimum.

The Baptism in the Holy Spirit may occur prior to the Baptism of Believers.

On one occasion the Lord sent Peter to a Gentile's house where he preached the message of Christ. While Peter was speaking to the Household of Cornelius, the Holy Spirit baptised them as they believed. Subsequently Peter instructed that they be baptised in water since they already received the baptism of the Holy Spirit.

Acts 10:44-48 (NKJV)
"44 While Peter was still speaking these words, the Holy Spirit fell upon all those who heard the word. 45 And those of the circumcision who believed were astonished, as many as came with Peter, *because the gift of the Holy Spirit had been poured out on the Gentiles also*. 46 For they heard them speak with tongues and magnify God. Then Peter answered, 47 "Can anyone forbid water, that *these should not be baptized who have received the Holy Spirit just as we have?*" 48 And *he commanded them to be baptized in the name of the Lord*. Then they asked him to stay a few days."

Just to be sure we have the story right, Peter explained the occurrences to the other Apostles when he returned to Jerusalem and then affirmed the order of how these gentile believers received the Baptism of the Holy Spirit, *"just as they did."*

Acts 11:15-17 (NKJV)
15 And as I began to speak, the Holy Spirit fell upon them, as upon us at the beginning. 16 Then I remembered *the word of the Lord, how He said,* 'John indeed baptized with water, *but you shall be baptized with the Holy Spirit.'* 17 *If therefore God gave them the same gift as He gave us when we believed on the Lord Jesus Christ*, who was I that I could withstand God?"

It was Peter's deep reverence for the Words of the Lord that consoled him and encouraged him to continue with these new Believers to also see that they be baptised in the Name of the Lord Jesus.

Let's talk about receiving the Holy Spirit for a few moments.

1. The Holy Spirit is a Person.

Jesus spoke about "He" in reference to the Holy Spirit in John 16 verses 13 to 14.

John 16:13-14 (NKJV)
"13 However, when **He**, the Spirit of truth, has come, *He will guide you* into all truth; for *He will not speak on His own authority*, but *whatever He hears He will speak*; and *He will tell you things to come.* 14 *He will glorify Me*, for *He will* take of what is Mine and *declare it to you*."

The Holy Spirit is ascribed with personality, influence and power. He is able to "guide", "speak," "hear," and "guide."

2. The Holy Spirit is from God and moved upon every one of the great men and woman of God in the Bible. He made the difference.

John 16:26 (NKJV)
"26 But the Helper, the Holy Spirit, ***whom the Father will send in My name***, He will teach you all things, and bring to your remembrance all things that I said to you."

We see that the Holy Spirit is sent from the Father. On many occasions in the Old Testament we read about "**the Spirit of the Lord**," meaning to say that the Holy Spirit is from God and He enabled ordinary people, to act in extra-ordinary ways. The Holy Spirit's Presence came with power and enablement, to those who had His power upon their lives.

Numbers 11:25 (NKJV)
"25 Then ***the Lord came down in the cloud***, and spoke to him, ***and took of the Spirit that was upon him, and placed the same upon the seventy elders***; and it happened, ***when the Spirit rested upon them, that they prophesied***, although they never did so again."

The Holy Spirit anointed people for specific Divine purposes.

Judges 6:34 (NKJV)
"34 But ***the Spirit of the Lord came upon Gideon***; then he blew the trumpet, and the Abiezrites gathered behind him."

King David was anointed by the Spirit of the Lord.

1 Samuel 16:13 (NKJV)
"13 Then Samuel took the horn of oil and anointed him in the midst of his brothers; and the Spirit of the Lord came upon David from that day forward. So Samuel arose and went to Ramah."

3. The Holy Spirit made the difference in Jesus' life and ministry.

Jesus declared in Luke 4 that "the Spirit of the Lord" was upon Him.

> Luke 4:18-19 (NKJV)
> "18 "The Spirit of the Lord is upon Me, Because He has anointed Me. To preach the gospel to the poor; He has sent Me to heal the brokenhearted, To proclaim liberty to the captives, And recovery of sight to the blind, To set at liberty those who are oppressed; 19 To proclaim the acceptable year of the Lord.""

> Acts 10:38 (NKJV)
> "38 how ***God anointed Jesus of Nazareth with the Holy Spirit and with power***, who went about ***doing good and healing all*** who were oppressed by the devil, ***for God was with Him***."

4. The Apostles experienced Him and ensured the Believers experienced Him.

The Apostles received the Baptism of the Holy Spirit first, however, from the very first message they preached, they encouraged Believers to desire and receive the Baptism of the Holy Spirit after being baptised.

> Acts 2:4 (NKJV)
> "4 And ***they were all filled with the Holy Spirit*** and began to speak with other tongues, as the Spirit gave them utterance."

> Acts 2:38-39 (NKJV)
> "38 Then Peter said to them, "Repent, and let every one of you be baptized in the name of Jesus Christ for the remission of

sins; and *you shall receive the gift of the Holy Spirit*. 39
For *the promise is to you and to your children, and to all
who are afar off, as many as the Lord our God will call*."

Acts 19:2, 6 (NKJV)
"..And finding some disciples 2 he said to them, "*Did you
receive the Holy Spirit when you believed?*" So they said
to him, "We have not so much as heard whether there is a
Holy Spirit." 6 And *when Paul had laid hands on them,
the Holy Spirit came upon them*, and they spoke with
tongues and prophesied."

There are a number of examples, even in the various pastoral
letters to the Churches.

The Holy Spirit empowers us to be His witnesses.

The Lord Jesus promised that we will receive "power" when the
Holy Spirit comes upon us, and through this "Power" of the Holy
Spirit, we will be His witnesses.

Acts 1:8 (NKJV)
"8 But *you shall receive power when the Holy Spirit has
come upon you*; and *you shall be witnesses* to Me in
Jerusalem, and in all Judea and Samaria, and to the end of
the earth."

The Holy Spirit empowers us to build one another up through His gifts.

God is no respecter of person and all His children are gifted by the
Holy Spirit with gifts. The purpose of these gifts is that they will serve
as instruments through which the Body of Christ will be built up,
strengthened and encouraged. The Baptism of the Holy Spirit opens
the doorway to these incredible gift.

1 Corinthians 12:7 (NKJV)
"7 But the manifestation of the Spirit is given to each one for
the profit of all"

1 Corinthians 12:11 (NKJV)
"11 But one and the same Spirit works all these things,
distributing to each one individually as He wills."

1 Peter 4:10 (NKJV)
"10 As each one has received a gift, minister it to one another,
as good stewards of the manifold grace of God."

My prayer is that each one of you will use those gifts on a daily basis to bring encouragement and hope to fellow Believers.

5. The Holy Spirit removes condemnation from those who walk under His direction.

Romans 8:1(NKJV)
"1 There is therefore now no condemnation to those who are in
Christ Jesus, who do not walk according to the flesh, but
according to the Spirit."

When we live in step with what the Spirit inside of us desire, then we live free from the condemnation of the law. The more we appropriate the Blood of Christ through the redemptive work of the Holy Spirit we find that the sense of forgiveness overrules the condemning thought and words around us.

6. The Holy Spirit enables us to walk in victory over the evil desires of our flesh.

Galatians 5:16 (NKJV)
"1 There is therefore now no condemnation to those who are in
Christ Jesus, who do not walk according to the flesh, but
according to the Spirit."

7. The Holy Spirit helps us to pray.

Romans 8:26-27 (NKJV)
"26 Likewise the Spirit also helps in our weaknesses. For we do
not know what we should pray for as we ought, but the
Spirit Himself makes intercession for us with groanings
which cannot be uttered. 27 Now He who searches the
hearts knows what the mind of the Spirit is, because He
makes intercession for the saints according to the will of
God."

This Scripture tells us that the Holy Spirit, if we allow Him, helps
us whilst we pray to pray according to the Will of God. He is an
amazing helper during our prayer times. He makes intercession for us.
How are you? Many times don't we know what to pray? Now we have a
Helper who is ready to intercede on our behalf whilst we remain in
prayer.

What happens when I receive the baptism of the Holy Spirit?

Evidences of Holy Spirit Baptism.

New Testament examples

In the New Testament we have a number of examples of when
Believers received the Baptism of the Holy Spirit. In the book of Acts,
the most common sign of Holy Spirit baptism was the speaking in
unknown tongues. In Jesus' final instructions to His Disciples, He
described to them the signs that will follow those who put their faith
in Him. One of the signs was that, "***they will speak with new
tongues.***"

Mark 16:17 (NKJV)
"17 And these signs will follow those who believe: In My name
they will cast out demons; ***they will speak with new
tongues;***"

So, it was no surprise to them that when they were all baptised in the Holy Spirit that they all spoke in other tongues.

In fact, of the five accounts we have in the Book of Acts, three explicitly describe the evidence of tongues, and other example, that of the Apostle Paul, by later revealed Scriptural knowledge, also spoke in tongues. Only one occasion does not make that distinction. Let's look at these occurrences.

1. The Apostles.

On the day of Pentecost, whilst they were all together in one accord, the Holy Spirit came upon all of them and baptised them all and they all spoke in other tongues as the Spirit gave them utterance.

> Acts 2:4 (NKJV)
> "4 And *they were all filled with the Holy Spirit and began to speak with other tongues*, as the Spirit gave them utterance."

2. New Believers in Samaria.

In Acts chapter 8 we read that the people in Samaria received the Word of God and were baptised in the Name of Jesus. The Apostles sent Peter and John from Jerusalem to these Believers to enquire whether they received the Baptism of the Holy Spirit. After speaking to them the Apostles laid their hands on them and they received the Holy Spirit. On this occasion we have no record of how they knew that they received the baptism of the Holy Spirit, apart from the Apostles reporting that they were. In my mind the evidence was clear to the Apostles so that they reported that they received the Holy Spirit.

> Acts 8:14-17 (NIV)
> "[14] When the apostles in Jerusalem heard that Samaria had accepted the word of God, they sent Peter and John to them. [15] When they arrived, *they prayed for them that*

they might receive the Holy Spirit, [16] because the Holy Spirit had not yet come upon any of them; they had simply been baptised into* the name of the Lord Jesus. [17] *Then Peter and John placed their hands on them, and they received the Holy Spirit*."

3. Saul of Tarsus (Apostle Paul)

In Acts 9 we read of how God sent Ananias to a certain street in Damascus to lay his hands on him to receive back his eye sight and to receive the in filling of the Holy Spirit.

> Acts 9:17-18 (NKJV)
> "17 And Ananias went his way and entered the house; and laying his hands on him he said, "Brother Saul, the Lord Jesus, who appeared to you on the road as you came, has sent me that you may receive your sight and be filled with the Holy Spirit." 18 Immediately there fell from his eyes something like scales, and he received his sight at once; and he arose and was baptized."

On this specific account there is no mention of him speaking in other tongues. However, when we look at what the Apostle write about in his letter to the church in Corinth, he confirms that He speaks in tongue, which allows one to draw the obvious conclusion that whether it is mentioned or not, there is an association between the Baptism of the Holy Spirit and speaking in tongues.

> 1 Corinthians 14:18 (NKJV)
> "18 I thank my God I speak with tongues more than you all;"

So, even though it did not specifically mention that Paul Spoke in tongues when he received the Baptism with the Holy Spirit, He nevertheless did.

4. Cornelius and His Household.

When God called Peter to go to the household of Cornelius, he did not expect these uncircumcised people to accept the Word of God and neither that they would be baptised in the Holy Spirit in the manner they did. While he was still speaking, the Holy Spirit baptised these Believers and they all spoke in tongues. How did the Apostles know that Cornelius and his household were baptised in the Holy Spirit? They heard them speaking in other tongues, just as they did when they received the Holy Spirit.

> Acts 10:44-48 (NIV)
> [44] While Peter was still speaking these words, the Holy Spirit came on all who heard the message. [45] The circumcised believers who had come with **Peter were astonished that the gift of the Holy Spirit had been poured out even on the Gentiles**. [46] **For they heard them speaking in tongues* and praising God.** Then Peter said, [47] "Can anyone keep these people from being baptised with water? **They have received the Holy Spirit just as we have.**" [48] So he ordered that they be baptised in the name of Jesus Christ. Then they asked Peter to stay with them for a few days."

This is an amazing account of gentiles receiving the Word of God, and being filled with the Holy Spirit.

5. Disciples at Ephesus.

The last account we read of in the Book of Acts is that from when the Apostle Paul went to Ephesus. Once again we have an account of people believing, without being baptised, and without receiving the Holy Spirit's Baptism at conversion. However, subsequent to some teaching, they were baptised in the Name of the Lord Jesus (Believers Baptism) and after Paul laid his hands on them, they received the baptism of the Holy Spirit.

Acts 19:1-7 (NIV) Paul in Ephesus [19:1] While Apollos was at Corinth, Paul took the road through the interior and arrived at Ephesus. There he found some disciples [2] and asked them, "Did you receive the Holy Spirit when you believed?" They answered, "No, we have not even heard that there is a Holy Spirit." [3] So Paul asked, "Then what baptism did you receive?" "John's baptism," they replied. [4] Paul said, "John's baptism was a baptism of repentance. He told the people to believe in the one coming after him, that is, in Jesus." [5] On hearing this, they were baptised into* the name of the Lord Jesus. [6] When Paul placed his hands on them, the Holy Spirit came on them, and they spoke in tongues* and prophesied. [7] There were about twelve men in all.

The Gifts of the Holy Spirit are for the upbuilding of the Church

Even though we've looked at these Scriptural examples, the apostle Paul says that not all will bring a message in tongues.

I Corinthians 12:30
"Are all apostles? Are all prophets? Are all teachers? Are all workers of miracles? Have all the gifts of healing? *do all speak with tongues*? do all interpret?"

There are nine gifts, or manifestations of the Spirit, and "diverse tongues" is just one of them.

I Corinthians 12:7-11
"But the manifestation of the Spirit is given to every man to profit withal. For to one is given by the Spirit the word of wisdom; to another the word of knowledge by the same Spirit; to another faith by the same Spirit; to another the gifts of healing by the same Spirit; to another the working of miracles; to another prophecy; to another discerning of spirits; to another divers kinds of tongues; to another the

interpretation of tongues: But all these worketh that one and the selfsame Spirit, *dividing to every man severally as he will.*"

Each of these nine gifts is a different manifestation of the same Spirit. Every believer has at least one spiritual gift, distributed by God as it pleases Him. *These gifts are given to edify the Body of Christ in love.*

Ephesians 4:16 (NIV 1984)
16 From him the whole body, joined and held together by every
   supporting ligament, grows and builds itself up in love, as
   each part does its work."

A believer must exercise faith in using his or her gift, because the gifts are initially undeveloped and must be exercised to grow and become fully mature over time. The goal, however, is not for us to be self-focused on our spiritual gifts, but to honor Jesus Christ and walk in His footsteps of humility and servanthood.

How can I receive the Baptism with the Holy Spirit?

I was a young teenager when I received the Baptism in the Holy Spirit on May 16, 1976. It happened before the service even started. We had a visiting Evangelist and his wife at our church that weekend. While Sister Stella Eilerd played some devotional music on the organ, before the service started, we were all in prayer, preparing our hearts to worship and to receive God's Word during the service that morning, I received the Baptism of the Holy Spirit. I spontaneously started speaking in tongues. It was as if there was a well of living waters inside of me welling up and out of me. I was overcome by the Holy Spirit. It was not disruptive or disturbing. It was an amazing experience. The Lord was there. Even though I never went through the waters of baptism before receiving the Baptism of the Holy Spirit, I soon afterwards was baptised.

My prayer is that you too will share and receive this wonderful promise from the Father. I want to share with you how I believe you might receive the Baptism of the Holy Spirit. Remember, this Promise is for you, who believe and were baptised.

1. Ask the Lord to baptise you with the Holy Spirit.

The first thing I encourage you to do is to ask the Father for His Holy Spirit. He promised the Holy Spirit to us as Believers. Believe and receive His promise!

> Luke 11:13 (NKJV)
> "13 If you then, being evil, know how to give good gifts to your children, *how much more will your heavenly Father give the Holy Spirit to those who ask Him*!""

Just as in this Scripture Jesus encourages us to ask, let us ask Him for the Baptism of the Holy Spirit, and believe that you will receive this promise of the Father.

> Hebrews 11:6 (NKJV)
> "6 But without faith it is impossible to please Him, for *he who comes to God must believe that He is, and that He is a rewarder of those who diligently seek Him*."

When we go to God, we must do so with faith in our hearts that He will hear us, and answer us, and reward us with Baptising us in the Holy Spirit, so ask the Lord for His Promise to you as a Believer, and you will receive the Gift the Father Promised.

> Acts 2:38-39 (NKJV) 38 Then Peter said to them, "*Repent, and let every one of you be baptized in the name of Jesus Christ* for the remission of sins; and *you shall receive the gift of the Holy Spirit*. 39 For *the promise is to you and to your children, and to all who are afar off, as many as the Lord our God will call*."

2. Drink from the fountain of Living waters.

The second thing I encourage you to do is to present yourself before God with an expectation, hungry and thirsty for the Living Water of His Spirit. Jesus, on one occasion, spoke about the Holy Spirit, and compared His presence within us to that of having a spring of Living water inside of us.

John 7:37-39 (NKJV)
"37 On the last day, that great day of the feast, Jesus stood and cried out, saying, "*If anyone thirsts, let him come to Me and drink.* 38 *He who believes in Me*, as the Scripture has said, *out of his heart will flow rivers of living water.*" 39 But this *He spoke concerning the Spirit, whom those believing in Him would receive*; for the Holy Spirit was not yet given, because Jesus was not yet glorified."

In this portion, Jesus communicated a few important things to us:

1. When we come to the Lord, we should come spiritually thirsty. He says in verse 37: "*If anyone thirsts, let him come to Me and drink.*" The source of the Holy Spirit is Jesus, and as we both come to Him and are thirsty for Him, we will receive the Holy Spirit; and
2. The Baptism of the Holy Spirit is for Believers. He says in verse 38 "*He who believes in Me,*" and then again in verse 39 "*whom those believing in Him would receive.*" If you know that you are a Believer and you are thirsty for the Living Water of the Holy Spirit, then your faith will be rewarded by a spring welling up from within you.
3. This whole portion was really a prophetic message that those who would put their faith in Jesus would receive the Baptism of the Holy Spirit, since the Apostle John tells us that: "*the Holy Spirit was not yet given, because Jesus was not yet glorified.*"

On one occasion Jesus spoke to a Samaritan woman and shared with her about this "**_Gift of God,_**" which we now know was in reference to the Holy Spirit, since He used similar language and analogy as the time He spoke on the last day of the feast. He used the analogy of "**_spring of living water,_**" and "**_welling up_**" from within them. He also connected the Believer to being "thirsty."

John 4:10 (NIV)
[10] Jesus answered her, "If you knew **_the gift of God_** and who it is that asks you for a drink, you would have asked him and he would have **_given you living water._**"

John 4:13-14 (NIV)
[13] Jesus answered, "Everyone who drinks this water will be thirsty again, [14] but **_whoever drinks the water I give him will never thirst_**. Indeed, **_the water I give him will become in him a spring of water welling up to eternal life._**"

I encourage you to drink of this "**_living water._**" Come into a place of worship where you close your eyes, to not be distracted by other things, and place your whole focus and expectation on Jesus, the Baptiser with the Holy Spirit. If you come "**_thirsty_**," I believe that your thirst will be quenched as Jesus Baptises you with His Holy Spirit. You too will experience this Spring of Living Waters welling up within you for the rest of your life.

3. Receive the Baptism of the Holy Spirit through the laying on of hands.

On a number of occasions we read, in the Book of Acts, that Believers received the Baptism of the Holy Spirit through the Laying on of hands. It does not always happen like this, but we most certainly see that the Baptism of the Holy Spirit was received on some occasions by this means. Through the years I have seen many people receive the Baptism of the Holy Spirit through the laying on of hands.

In the next part of this course we will look at this "laying on of hands' more specifically. We see that Peter and John placed their hands on the Believers in Samaria, and they received the Holy Spirit. We also the Apostle Paul lay his hands on the Believers in Ephesus and they received the Baptism of the Holy Spirit.

> Acts 8:17(NKJV)
> "17 Then they laid hands on them, and they received the Holy
> Spirit."

> Acts 19:6 (NKJV)
> "6 And when Paul had laid hands on them, the Holy Spirit came
> upon them, and they spoke with tongues and prophesied."

As I mentioned earlier, I received the Baptism of the Holy Spirit, before a service actually started, during a time of prayer, and preparing my heart to receive His Word. We have examples, such as was the case when Peter spoke to the household of Cornelius, that while he was still speaking, the people received the baptism of the Holy Spirit.

4. Receive the Baptism of the Holy Spirit while worshipping and praying.

Prayer and Worship are two of the most powerful atmosphere settings you could position yourself in to receive the Baptism of the Holy Spirit. Put on some worship music, or go to a gathering of Believers where true worship or devotional music is sang or played, and while you are worshipping, trust the Lord to fill you with that "***Living water.***"

I have heard of many Believers receiving the baptism of the Holy Spirit while they were praying. In fact, on the Day of Pentecost, the Disciples were together, "in one accord," and while they were in this place of spiritual unity, possibly praying, they receive the Baptism of the Holy Spirit. Acts 2 verse 2 says they were "sitting," a position of lowliness and submission in the Presence of the Lord.

Acts 1:14 (NKJV)

"14 ***These all continued with one accord in prayer and supplication***, with the women and Mary the mother of Jesus, and with His brothers."

Acts 2:1 (NKJV)

"1 When the Day of Pentecost had fully come, ***they were all with one accord in one place.***"

Acts 2:2 (NKJV)

"2 And suddenly there came a sound from heaven, as of a rushing mighty wind, and it filled the whole house where ***they were sitting.***"

I believe that being in a prayerful and worshipful atmosphere, and attitude, will position you favourably to receive the Baptism of the Holy Spirit.

What will happen to you?

1. You might start to speak in tongues.
2. You might be overcome with emotion as the Holy Spirit fills you. It is not an emotion of sadness, but one of joy and amazement.
3. You might start to boldly prophecy, by speaking the Word of God over people's lives, uncharacteristic to how you would normally behave.
4. You might start to sing a new song of praise and exultation to the Lord. It will not bother you since it will be like something has come over you and it will just well up from within you. You will truly experience the spring of living water welling up from within.
5. You might experience exceeding joy and gladness as you as submersed, in a sense, in the Power of the Holy Spirit.

I pray that you will share this wonderful promise of the Father.

ASSIMILATION SHEET
BAPTISMS

1. Complete the sentence. *The first Baptism, is a baptism into the* **Body** *of Christ.*

2. Complete the sentence: *"Whoever believes and is* **baptized** *will be saved."*

3. What Promise from the Father did Peter present to those who repented and were baptised, according to Acts 2:37-38?

   Peter told the people that they would receive the Baptism of the Holy Spirit.

4. Complete the sentence. *The Biblical method of Baptism is by* **immersion**.

5. **What happens when we are baptised, according to Romans 6?**

   1. Into the water, speaks of **death** unto self.
   2. Out of the water, speaks of **resurrection** to a new life, and **clothing** one self with Christ.

PART IV

LAYING ON OF HANDS

The Laying on of Hands is an extremely important foundation to establish in the life of a Believer. God is Mighty and His Power and Authority is Supreme, yet one of the amazing things of this Mighty God is, that He chooses to use people through whom He speaks and ministers. The Laying on of hands is that ministry that takes places where God touches others, through His commissioned servants, to commission certain people for specific divine purposes, to make conciliation, to bring healing to the sick, and to bestow gifts, especially the Gift of the Holy Spirit.

Throughout the Old Testament we see that *the laying on of hands was practiced in the commissioning of people for divine service and purposes*. On all occasions *the laying on of hands came from a direct instruction from the Lord*, and it should therefor always be upheld and honoured as such as we practice this in the Church.

Let's take for instance the example from Numbers 27 when God said to Moses to commission Joshua as his successor. We see that the instruction came from the Lord.

Numbers 27:18-20 (NKJV)

"18 And **the Lord said to Moses**: "Take Joshua the son of Nun with you, a man in whom is the Spirit, **and lay your hand on him**; 19 **set him before Eleazar the priest and before all the congregation, and inaugurate him in their sight.** 20 **And you shall give some of your authority to him,** that all the congregation of the children of Israel may be obedient."

Numbers 27:23 (NKJV)

"23 **And he laid his hands on him and inaugurated him, just as the Lord commanded by the hand of Moses.**"

Deuteronomy 34:9 (NKJV)

"9 **Now Joshua** the son of Nun **was full of the spirit of wisdom, for Moses had laid his hands on him**; so the **children of Israel heeded him**, and did as the Lord had commanded Moses."

We learn from this "Laying on of hands," that Joshua was inaugurated, and received authority and the "spirit of wisdom." We see that every verse confirmed that the instruction came from the Lord, and the "Laying on of Hands" happened "before all the congregation." We also learn from these portion of Scriptures that the congregation "heeded" and "obeyed" these commissioned leaders. This is a Holy Ordinance which should be done 1. Under the direct instruction of the Lord, and 2. In the presence of all the congregation, who will 3. Willingly adhered to their instructions as unto the Lord. Of course some have misused this Divine Commissioning, yet we are called upon to lay this foundation in our faith.

This practice was strongly upheld and regarded in the early Church, and should be upheld in the church and among Believers today. When the early Church elected Spirit-filled Deacons to help with the ministry of serving, the Apostles laid their hands on them and commissioned them for that purpose in the presence of the whole church.

Acts 6:3-6 (NKJV)

"3 Therefore, brethren, seek out from among you seven men of good reputation, full of the Holy Spirit and wisdom, *whom we may appoint over this business*; 4 but we will give ourselves continually to prayer and to the ministry of the word." 5 And the saying pleased the whole multitude. And *they chose Stephen*, a man full of faith and the Holy Spirit, and *Philip, Prochorus, Nicanor, Timon, Parmenas, and Nicolas*, a proselyte from Antioch, 6 *whom they set before the apostles; and when they had prayed, they laid hands on them.*"

We have this other example in the church in Antioch, when the Holy Spirit commissioned Barnabas and Saul (the Apostle Paul) for a specific mission, and here we see again, after prayer and fasting, the church leaders who were present, under the instruction of the Holy Spirit, commissioning them by the laying on of hands.

Acts 13:3 (NKJV)

"1 Now in the church that was at Antioch there were *certain prophets and teachers*: Barnabas, Simeon who was called Niger, Lucius of Cyrene, Manaen who had been brought up with Herod the tetrarch, and Saul. 2 *As they ministered to the Lord and fasted, the Holy Spirit said*, "Now *separate to Me Barnabas and Saul for the work to which I have called them.*" 3 Then, *having fasted and prayed, and laid hands on them, they sent them away.*"

It is this "*laying on of hands*" that was honoured and regarded in the early church, both by the people who were "commissioned" and "anointed" for their "higher calling" and service, and by those who observed the 'Laying on of Hands." These men and woman were held in high regard, since the Lord set them apart by the "laying on of hands" for their service.

1 Thessalonians 5:12-13 (NIV)

"[12] Now we ask you, brothers, *to respect those who work hard among you, who are over you in the Lord and who admonish you.* [13] *Hold them in the highest regard in love because of their work.* Live in peace with each other."

Hebrews 13:17 (NIV)

[17] *Obey your leaders and submit to their authority.* They keep watch over you as men who must give an account. *Obey them so that their work will be a joy*, not a burden, for that would be of no advantage to you.

The foundation of the "laying on of hands," and upholding it in our lives is therefor in one sense an honouring of the Lord's choosing of men and woman to lead in the affairs of the church, and an honouring of the "anointing" that comes as a result of this "laying on of hands." We show that we value this foundation in our lives when we honour those whom the Lord set aside for specific purposes and upon whom hands were laid in the presence of God and the congregation. Without valuing this foundation, we wont value the setting aside of some for spiritual purpose, and neither will we value their appointment over us. With valuing the Foundation of "laying on of hands" come both a respect for those on whom hands have been laid as well as for the position in which God placed them.

Be careful to not lay hands on people too quickly!

In the appointment of Elders, and I think for any appointment in the church, we need to take care that we are not too haste in "laying hands on people," but to let them first prove themselves and show by their godly lives that they are worthy of receiving such "laying on of hands" in service to the Lord.

1 Timothy 5:22 (NKJV)

"22 *Do not lay hands on anyone hastily*, nor share in other people's sins; keep yourself pure."

I wish to exhort you to value the "laying on of hands" as something to be done carefully and only under instruction and guidance of the Lord, since it is ultimately His conference of power and authority that legitimises the action. Do so under His guidance and instruction.

Pardoning of <u>sins</u> came from the laying on of hands.

Another example of the "laying on of hands" came from the instruction of the Lord to the priests, whom He instructed to lay their hands on the various offerings, to receive it on His behalf, and to confer on those animals the sins and offences of the people. The laying on of hands was that action by which transfer took place.

Leviticus 1:4 (NKJV)
"4 Then ***he shall put his hand on the head of the burnt offering, and it will be accepted on his behalf to make atonement for him.***"

In this Scripture and a number more in the Book of Leviticus, we see that pardon would come when the Priest confer the sin of the confessing sinner, through the laying on of hands, onto the offering they present before the Priest, and therefor before God.

<u>Healing</u> came through the laying on of hands.

In the New Testament we find that Christ laid His hands on the sick and they got well.

Luke 4:40 (NIV 1984)
"40 When the sun was setting, the people brought to Jesus all who had various kinds of sickness, and ***laying his hands on each one, he healed them.***"

Jesus encouraged and instructed Believers to lay their hands on the sick so that they will recover.

Mark 16:18 (NKJV)

"18 they will take up serpents; and if they drink anything deadly, it will by no means hurt them; *they will lay hands on the sick, and they will recover.*""

Spiritual <u>gifts</u> are imparted through the laying on Hands.

The early Church placed a high value on the Apostles laying hands on them. It was regarded and received as if it was the Lord Himself laying His Hand on them. The Laying on of Hands was and is a powerful tool in the Hands of God to bring healing, impart Spiritual Gifts, and to set people apart for service unto the Lord.

Acts 8:17-19 (NIV)

17 Then ***Peter and John placed their hands on them, and they received the Holy Spirit.*** 18 When Simon saw that the Spirit was given at the laying on of the apostles' hands, he offered them money 19 and said, "Give me also this ability so that everyone on whom I lay my hands may receive the Holy Spirit."

2 Timothy 1:6 (NIV)

"*6 For this reason I remind you to **fan into flame the gift of God, which is in you through the laying on of my hands.***"

The use of the '***Laying on of Hands***" is therefor something to be ***treated with the utmost respect and reverence.*** We, on God's behalf, and under His instruction, lay our hands on people to impart blessing, pardon, healing or some Spiritual Gift or empowerment. These should be practiced with care and consideration. On the other hand, we show the value we place on God's choosing of servants, by honouring and obeying those who administer such "laying on of Hands," on His behalf.

ASSIMILATION SHEET

LAYING ON OF HANDS

1. Complete the sentence. *The laying on of hands was practiced in the commissioning of people for **divine** service and purposes.*

2. Complete the sentence. *The laying on of hands came from a direct instruction from the **Lord**.*

3. Name two blessings that came on Joshua as a result of Moses laying his hands on him, according to Numbers 27 and Deuteronomy 34?
   Joshua received the spirit of Wisdom and He received the same Authority that rested on Moses.

4. Where should the laying on of hands take place? *The laying on of Hands should take place in the presence of the Lord and the Congregation.*

5. Give two New Testament examples of this laying on of hands, in the commissioning for service? *We have the example from when Paul and Barnabas was sent out by the Church In Antioch, and we have the example of when the Apostles laid their hands on the Deacons, who were chosen by the congregation, to serve as Deacons.*

6. Luke 4:40 give us an example of some spiritual gift that operates through the laying on of hands. Which spiritual gift do you see being used? *Jesus laid His Hands on the sick people, and they received their healing. The Gift of Healing operated here.*

7. Acts 8:17-19 gives us another example of some spiritual activity through the laying on of hands. What happened here to the Believers through the laying on of hands? *We see that they received the Baptism of the Holy Spirit through the laying on of hands.*

PART V

THE RESURRECTION OF THE DEAD.

The Resurrection of the dead is an essential constituent of our faith in Christ. Through embracing this truth, about the resurrection, we embrace the fact that 1. Christ rose from the dead, as He said He would, and 2. We too will rise again, either for eternal life, or unto eternal damnation.

Since Christ rose from the <u>dead</u>, we embrace the Resurrection of the dead.

One of the essentials teachings we as Believers embrace is the teaching on the "**Resurrection of the Dead.**" Our entire Gospel hinges on the fact that **Jesus rose from the dead**. He is Alive, and through Him we can truly embrace eternal life!

1 Corinthians 15:20-21 (NIV)
"*20 But Christ has indeed been raised from the dead, the firstfruits of those who have fallen asleep. 21 For **since death came through a man, the resurrection of the dead comes also through a man**.*"

Since Christ died and rose from the dead our new **birth** is assured and affirmed. There is a direct connection between the resurrection of Christ and our New Birth. His Resurrection provides us with a living Hope of our New Birth.

1 Peter 1:3 (NIV)
*"3 Praise be to the God and Father of our Lord Jesus Christ! In his great mercy **he has given us new birth into a living hope through the resurrection of Jesus Christ from the dead**,"*

Since Christ rose from the dead, we too shall rise from the dead to eternal life.

Every Believer should live daily with this eternal hope in his or her heart, since Christ rose from the dead, we too shall rise from the dead to eternal life. When Jesus comes back, He is coming to fetch us, His children, to be with Him for eternity. We should live with this eternal hope in our hearts.

1 Thessalonians 4:16 (NIV 1984)
"16 For the Lord himself will come down from heaven, with a loud command, with the voice of the archangel and with the trumpet call of God, and **the dead in Christ will rise first**."

Every Believer lives with this Eternal Hope in his or her heart, that we who are in Christ will rise again. We will also experience this resurrection Power in our lives when Christ returns.

By embracing the Resurrection of the dead we embrace eternal life.

Christ came to give all who believe in Him, eternal life. The essence of eternal life is that, even if we die before His second coming, we will rise again from the dead. There is life after death.

John 3:14-16 (NKJV)

"14 And as Moses lifted up the serpent in the wilderness, even so must the Son of Man be lifted up, 15 that *whoever believes in Him should not perish but have eternal life*. 16 For God so loved the world that He gave His only begotten Son, *that whoever believes in Him should not perish but have everlasting life*."

1 Corinthians 15:12-14 (NIV 1984)

"12 *But if it is preached that Christ has been raised from the dead, how can some of you say that there is no resurrection of the dead. 13 If there is no resurrection of the dead, then not even Christ has been raised. 14 And if Christ has not been raised, our preaching is useless and so is your faith.*"

God so loved us that He sent His Son, Jesus Christ, to die on the cross that we could have eternal life through faith in Him. The life we now live has eternal consequences of which we need to be aware of. By embracing Jesus Christ, we embrace the resurrection of the dead, meaning that we embrace a commitment to live this life in such a way that we will be able to stand before that Throne one day and be counted among those in whom He will be well pleased.

By embracing the Resurrection of the dead we embrace the second coming of Christ.

Jesus is coming back again, and we as believers should live as those who expect to stand before Him one day and give account of our life on earth. We will be without excuse on that day since Christ paid a high price to pave the way for us to have eternal life.

Matthew 25:31-32 (NKJV)

"31 *"When the Son of Man comes in His glory, and all the holy angels with Him, then He will sit on the throne of His glory. 32 All the nations will be gathered before Him, and He will separate them one from another,* as a shepherd divides his sheep from the goats."

Matthew 25:34 (NKJV)
"34 Then the King will say to **those on His right hand**, '*Come, you blessed of My Father, inherit the kingdom prepared for you from the foundation of the world:*"

Matthew 25:41(NKJV)
"41 "Then He will also say to **those on the left hand**, '*Depart from Me, you cursed, into the everlasting fire prepared for the devil and his angels:*"

Matthew 25:46 (NKJV)
"*46 And these will go away into everlasting punishment, but the righteous into eternal life.*""

What are the key points for us to understand and appreciate?

The key points are that the way we live in this life has eternal consequences. **We will all rise from the dead, whether we were Believers or not.** The Believers will rise unto eternal **life** and the unbelievers unto eternal **damnation**. This brings us to our next session on Eternal judgment.

2 Peter 3:10-14 (NIV 1984)
"*10 But the day of the Lord will come like a thief. The heavens will disappear with a roar; the elements will be destroyed by fire, and the earth and everything in it will be laid bare. 11 Since everything will be destroyed in this way, what kind of people ought you to be? You ought to live holy and godly lives 12 as you look forward to the day of God and speed its coming. That day will bring about the destruction of the heavens by fire, and the elements will melt in the heat. 13 But in keeping with his promise we are looking forward to a new heaven and a new earth, the home of righteousness. 14 So*

then, dear friends, since you are looking forward to this, make every effort to be found spotless, blameless and at peace with him."

ASSIMILATION SHEET
RESURRECTION OF THE DEAD

1. Complete the sentence. *By embracing the Resurrection of the dead we embrace the fact that* **Christ** *was the first to rise from the* **dead**.

2. Complete the sentence. *1 Corinthians 15:20-21 (NIV 1984) tells us: "20 But Christ has indeed been* **raised** *from the dead, the* **firstfruits** *of those who have fallen asleep. 21 For* **since death came through a man, the resurrection of the dead** comes **also through a man.**"*

3. Complete the sentence. *Since Christ rose from the dead,* **we** *too shall rise from the dead to* **eternal life**.

4. Complete the sentence. *By embracing the Resurrection of the dead we embrace the* **second coming** *of Christ.*

5. Who will rise from the dead? *The dead in Christ will rise, when Jesus return.*

6. Consider 2 Peter 3:10-14 for a moment. What kind of lives do we need to live as we expect His return?

We need to live holy and godly lives. We need to live lives that are blameless, spotless, and at peace with Him.

PART VI

ETERNAL JUDGMENT

The early Church counted it an essential firm foundation to establish in the daily life of every new Believer: *the consciousness of eternal consequences*. **The reward for our sins should be death on a cross.** Christ made it possible that we could escape that eternal judgment by believing in Him, however, this faith should be reflected in the way in which we value His propitiation for our sins. The life we now live should be consistent with our eternal gratitude.

John 3:16 (NIV 1984)
"16 *"For God so loved the world that he gave his one and only Son, that* ***whoever believes in him shall not perish but have eternal life.***"

Romans 14:10 (NIV 1984)
"10 *You, then, why do you judge your brother? Or why do you look down on your brother? For* ***we will all stand before God's judgment seat.***"

As people who will stand before our Lord, every Believer should embrace the following heart attitude:

1. We need to live with a <u>daily</u> awareness that at the end of our lives <u>we will</u> stand before the Throne of God, and give account of <u>ourselves</u>, to God.

Romans 14:12 (NIV 1984)
*"12 So then, **<u>each</u> of us will give an account of himself** to God."*

Sometimes people <u>forget</u> that we will all give an account of <u>ourselves</u> to God. Many people live as if they are beyond having to give account. Be reminded that it was Christ who forewarned us of this day of accounting. When we harness ourselves with this mindfulness of eternal judgment, we will constantly adjust and consider our ways in view of our appearing before our King. This should not only be seen from a negative point of view but also from a positive view. I'm sure you also live to please the One who saved you. I want to stand before Him and hear those amazing words: "***Welcome home, and well done, good, and <u>faithful</u> servant!***" Let us live with this eternal expectation of our just reward in our hearts.

2. We need to <u>live</u> our lives as those who <u>will</u> have to give account for our actions.

The fact remains that ***our words and <u>actions</u> are important and has a bearing on how we will spend <u>eternity</u>***. One of the constant and consistent messages of the Lord Jesus to His Disciples, and then from the Apostles to the Believers in the various Churches, was the message that our faith and walk need to be consistent with the faith we profess.

Jesus one day spoke to some Scribes and Pharisees about this consistency between what people profess and the fruit they bear with their lives. He made the direct comparison with us. He said that: " (NKJV) ***a tree is known by its <u>fruit</u>,***" *and then* "***How can you, being evil, speak good things? For out of the abundance of the <u>heart</u> the mouth speaks.***"

These words challenged them to consider their ways, and challenges us to consider our ways. We are all on public display daily. Our lives tell a story. He went on to bring this message home by telling us that we will give account *"for every idle word"* we speak in *"the day of judgement."*

Matthew 12:36-37 (NKJV)
"36 But I say to you that *for every idle word men may speak, they will give account of it in the day of judgment*. 37 For by your <u>words</u> you will be justified, and by your <u>words</u> you will be condemned.""

As Believers, our words should be <u>considered</u> before we utter them. May the Lord help you to put aside the language of the world. I have seen, through the years, how the language of new Believers becomes one of the first signs to their unbelieving friends that things have changed. We see that the crudeness and swearing stops, the negativity is replaced with positiveness, and the lying and deceit is replaced with honestly, respect and kindness. May this be your testimony as well.

James 2:21-24 (NIV)
"[21] Was not our ancestor Abraham considered righteous for what he did when he offered his son Isaac on the altar? [22] *You see that his faith and his actions were working together*, and his faith was made complete **by what he <u>did</u>.** [23] And the scripture was fulfilled that says, "Abraham believed God, and it was credited to him as righteousness," and he was called God's friend. [24] *You see that a person is justified by what he <u>does</u> and <u>not</u> by faith alone.*"

James 2:12 (NKJV)
"12 *So <u>speak</u> and so <u>do</u> as those who will be judged* by the law of liberty."

Colossians 4:5-6 (NIV) "[5] *Be wise in the way you act toward outsiders*; make the most of every opportunity. [6] *Let your conversation be always full of grace*, seasoned with salt, so that you may know how to answer everyone."

We will explore more on the things we need to clothe ourselves with as Believers in another session, but for now it is important to build into our spiritual DNA the awareness that our actions, deeds and words both tell of the change which Christ brought in us as well as bring testimony to His Grace extended in us. Our lives bear witness to the life of Christ in us. May this changed life bear witness unto eternity.

3. We need to be Faithful Servants, doing what God called us to do.

One day Jesus told His Disciples a Parable on stewardship. He told them of a certain master who gave each one of his servants, talents to use. After a long while He returned and required them to give account of the talents they received. When you read this parable in Matthew 25, you quickly notice the message of how Jesus requires us to use our talents and produce a harvest. May the Lord grant that you and I use our talents to full use so that we may produce a multiplied harvest when He returns.

Matthew 25:20-21(NKJV)
"20 "So he who had received five talents came and brought five other talents, saying, 'Lord, you delivered to me five talents; look, I have gained five more talents besides them.' 21 His lord said to him, '*Well done, good and Faithful servant; you were Faithful over a few things, I will make you ruler over many things. Enter into the joy of your lord.*'"

I want to stand before the Lord and hear those wonderful words: "*Well done, good and faithful servant.*"

Ephesians 2:10 (NKJV) "10 For we are His workmanship, created in Christ Jesus for good works, which God prepared beforehand that we should walk in them."

1 Peter 4:10-11 (NKJV) "10 ***As each one has received a gift, minister it to one another, as good stewards of the manifold grace of God.*** 11 If anyone speaks, let him speak as the oracles of God. If anyone ministers, let him do it as with the ability which God supplies, that in all things God may be glorified through Jesus Christ, to whom belong the glory and the dominion forever and ever. Amen."

The reason I emphasise this aspect so much, is for us to build a solid foundation in our spiritual lives, which will carry us through to that Day when we stand before Him, so that we can stand before Him with joy and not be ashamed.

4. Eternal judgement also brings eternal rewards.

The God we serve is into the giving of rewards and rewarding His children. When He comes again, he is coming with His reward with Him. ***Eternal Judgement should not only be seen as place of negative reckoning but rather as a place where our lives, our actions and deeds, will be assesses and where we will receive our just reward.*** There are wonderful servants of the Lord, some have passed away already, who have endured a lot for the sake of the Gospel. This Day will be a day where we will all receive our reward.

Revelation 22:12 (NKJV)
"12 "And behold, I am coming quickly, and My reward is with Me, to give to everyone according to his work."

1 Corinthians 3:8 (NKJV)
"8 Now he who plants and he who waters are one, and each one will receive his own reward according to his own labor."

1 Corinthians 3:12-14 (NKJV)

"12 Now if anyone builds on this foundation with gold, silver, precious stones, wood, hay, straw, 13 each one's <u>work</u> will become clear; for the Day will declare it, because it will be revealed by fire; and the <u>fire</u> will test each one's work, of what sort it is. 14 If anyone's work which he has built on it <u>endures</u>, he will receive a reward."

Live with this internal reference point in you always. Jesus is coming back again, and this time He is coming to reward the faithful, the humble, the persevering, and those who truly believed Him and His Word. May you too be counted among them who will receive their just reward for righteous living.

ASSIMILATION SHEET
ETERNAL JUDGEMENT

1. Complete the sentence. *The early Church, counted it an essential, firm foundation, to establish in the daily life of every new Believer:* **the consciousness of eternal consequences**.

2. Complete the sentence. *The reward for our sins should be* **death** *on a* **cross**.

3. Complete the sentence. *We need to live with a daily awareness that at the end of our lives we will stand before the* **Throne of God**, *and give account of* **ourselves**, *to God.*

4. Who will give account to God? *We will all give account of ourselves to God.*

5. *"We need to live our lives as those who will have to give account for our actions."* What does this mean to you? *It means that we need to live with a constant awareness that our thoughts, words, and actions have a direct impact on How we will spend eternity.*

6. Does our words and actions have any effect on how we will spend eternity? Yes

If Yes, give me one Scripture to substantiate your belief. Matthew 12:36-37

7. Is it important for our faith and actions to be consistent? Yes.

If Yes, what portion of Scripture, best describes this from our lesson? James 2:21-24

8. How can we tell that someone have been Born again? We know that someone is born again by the way they speak, act and behave.

9. Is this true in your life? *YES!*

If Yes, give me an example of things that have changed, and that is consistently, observably different in your life now, since you committed your life to Christ? _____

_____

9. If there is a reward for faithful stewardship and living, what is the reward for disobedience and slothfulness? *The reward for disobedience and slothfulness is eternal damnation.*

PART VII

CONCLUSION ON THE SIX FOUNDATIONAL PRINCIPLES:

As you will discover in days, weeks, months and years to come, the Bible is filled with reinforcement of these foundational principles towards Godly living.

When we look at the teachings of Jesus, we see that His teaching started with Him teaching His disciples about the values of the Kingdom. We all live in a certain culture. A culture is the shared embracing of values. Jesus came to establish the Kingdom of God. Each kingdom has its own culture. When we become children of God, we transition from the Kingdom of this world to the Kingdom of our Lord and Saviour, Jesus Christ. The Kingdom of God has its own culture. The first thing we need to learn as Believers and as Followers of Jesus Christ is how to adopt the culture of the Kingdom of God.

A few years ago we migrated from South Africa to Australia. It was quite a process, one that I don't recommend to the faint-hearted. Once our qualifications, health checks and police clearances were accessed and accepted, we were granted residency visas in Australia, however, when we wanted to become Citizens, we were required to learn, adopt, and accept the cultural values of the Australian people. This is an appropriate and acceptable practice in the kingdoms of this world, and it should be even more so as people migrate their affections from the earthly to the heavenly, from the kingdom of the world to the Kingdom of God. It is equally, if not more, important to assimilate the values of the Kingdom of God when we become children of God.

Jesus started discipling His Disciples by teaching them the Kingdom Values. The reason He started here, and not with first laying a Salvation Foundation, was that He taught people who already left everything and made a tangible commitment to follow Him. He taught people who committed themselves already.

When Jesus discipled His disciples, He seemed to follow a specific pathway over the three and a half years He was with them. The Gospels give us insight into parts of this process of how they were Discipled. I believe we could gain a lot of insight if we learn the key elements of what Jesus taught His Disciples. For me it is important, in developing a Biblical process of Discipleship, to follow the example of Jesus as far as possible, and to teach them everything He taught us. Discipleship Two will explore the Values of the Kingdom of God.

OTHER BOOKS OF DR. HENDRIK J VORSTER

Step One - Salvation Disciple Manual

Discipleship Foundation Series
Step One - Salvation

This Course explores the "How to" be Born Again and to establish a solid Foundation for your faith in Jesus Christ. It is based on Hebrews chapter 6 verses 1 and 2, and explores:

    Repentance of dead works,
    Faith in God,
    Baptisms,
    Laying on of hands,
    Resurrection of the dead, and
    Eternal Judgement

Free Video Teaching material is available at www.discipleshipcourses.com ***Disciple Manuals can be purchased*** through our website: www.churchplantinginstitute.com or at www.amazon.com

Step Two - Values and Spiritual Disciplines Disciple Manual

Discipleship Foundations Series Step Two - Values and Spiritual Disciplines Disciple Manual

By Dr. Hendrik J Vorster

This Course explores the *"How to" develop spiritual disciplines* as well as *52 Values* Jesus taught. It is based on the teachings of Jesus to His Disciples, and explores:

Spiritual Disciplines

The disciplines we explore are: Reading, meditating on the Word of God, Prayer, Stewardship, Fasting, Servanthood, Simplicity, Worship, and Witnessing.

Values of the Kingdom of God

Humility, Mournfulness, meekness, Spiritual Passion, Mercifulness, Purity, Peacemaker, Patient endurance, Example, Custodian, Reconciliatory, Resoluteness, Loving, Discreetness, Forgiving, Kingdom of God Investor, God-minded, Kingdom of God prioritiser, Introspective, Persistent, Considerate, Conservative, Fruit-bearing, Practitioner, Accountability, Faithful, Childlikeness, Unity, Servanthood, Loyalty, Gratefulness, Stewardship, Obedience, Carefulness, Compassion, Caring, Confidence, Steadfastness, Contentment, Teachable, Deference, Diligence, Trustworthiness, Gentleness, Discernment, Truthfulness, Generous, Kindness, Watchfulness, Perseverance, Honouring and Submissive.

This, Disciple Manual and Video Teaching materials are available, for purchase, from www.discipleshipcourses.com our website: www.churchplantinginstitute.com or at www.amazon.com

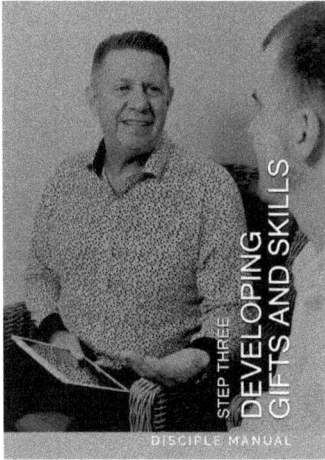

Step Three - Developing Gifts and Skills

Discipleship Foundations Series Step Three - Developing Gifts and Skills

This course is run through *five weekend encounters*. These weekend encounters have been designed to help Disciples discover their spiritual gifts, as well as learn skills to use their gifts, and to serve the Lord for the extension of His Kingdom. The Weekend Encounters are:

Gifts Discovery Encounter

We learn about Ministerial Office gifts, Service gifts, and Supernatural Spiritual Gifts. We discover our own, and then learn How we may use them to build up the local Church.

Survey of the Bible Weekend Encounter

During this weekend we do a survey of the Bible, from Genesis to Revelation. We also learn about the History of the Bible as well as How we can make most of our time in the Word.

Sharing your Faith Weekend Encounter

During this weekend we learn about the Gospel message, and *How to share our faith* effectively.

Overcoming Weekend Encounter

During this weekend we deal with those *thistles and thorns* that smother the growth and harvest of the good seed sown into our lives. We address How to overcome fear, unforgiveness, lust and the cares of the world with faith and obedience.

Shepherd Leader Weekend Encounter

During this weekend encounter we learn about being a Good Shepherd, and How to best disciple in a small group.

This, Disciple Manual and Video Teaching materials are available, for purchase, from www.discipleshipcourses.com our website: www.churchplantinginstitute.com or at www.amazon.com

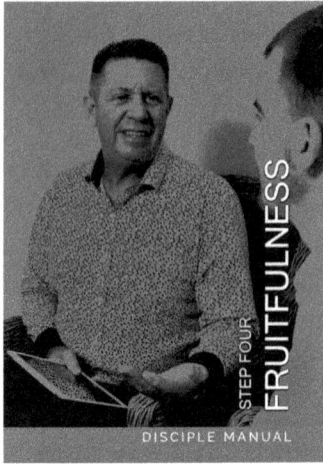

Step Four - Fruitfulness

Discipleship Foundations Series Step Four - Discipling Fruit-Producers

By Dr. Hendrik J Vorster

We were saved to serve. This course has been designed to mobilise Believers, from Learners to Practitioners. These sessions have been prepared for individual use, with those who are bearing fruit, and want to produce more fruit. Developing these areas in a sustained and systematic manner will ensure both fruitfulness and multiplication. Attending to these areas will ensure that you bear lasting fruit.

We explore:

1. Introduction.
2. Walking with purpose.
3. Build purposeful relationships. Finding Worthy Men
4. Priesthood. Praying effectively for those entrusted to you.
5. Caring compassionately.
6. Walking worthily.
7. Walking in the Spirit.
8. Practicing hospitality.

This, Disciple Manual and Video Teaching materials are available, for purchase, from www.discipleshipcourses.com our website: www.churchplantinginstitute.com or at www.amazon.com

Step Five - Multiplication - Dr. Hendrik J Vorster

Discipleship Foundations Series
Step Five - Multiplication

By Dr Hendrik J Vorster

This course was designed to assist fruit-producing disciples to live a life that will encourage a lifetime of fruitfulness. It will also give our disciples skills and guidelines to navigate their disciples through seasons of challenge and growth. This course is packed with Leadership advancing principles. The more these areas are addressed and encouraged, the more we will experience growth and multiplication.

We explore:

1. Vision and dreams.
2. Set Godly Goals.
3. Character development
4. Gifts development - Impartation and Activation
5. Fruitfulness comes through constant challenge.
6. Relationships - Family, Children and Friends
7. The Power of encouragement
8. Finances - Personal and Ministry finances
9. Dealing with setbacks
- *How to deal with failure?*
- *How to deal with betrayal?*
- *How to deal with rejection?*
- *How to deal with trials?*
- *How to deal with despondency?*
10. Eternal rewards

This, Disciple Manual and Video Teaching materials are available, for purchase, from www.discipleshipcourses.com our website: www.churchplantinginstitute.com or at www.amazon.com

Values
of the
Kingdom
of
God

Dr. Hendrik J. Vorster

Values of the Kingdom of God - Dr Hendrik J Vorster

**SPIRITUAL
DISCIPLINES**
OF THE
KINGDOM
OF
GOD

Spiritual Disciplines of the Kingdom of God - Dr Hendrik J Vorster

Values of the Kingdom of God
By Dr. Hendrik J Vorster

Everyone desires to be known as a pleasant to be around with kind of person. This book helps you develop values towards such a godly character. This book explores 52 Values of the Kingdom of God.

These **Books** are available from: www.churchplantinginstitute.com or at www.amazon.com

Spiritual Disciplines of the Kingdom of God
By Dr. Hendrik J Vorster

Every Believer desires to be a Fruit-producing branch in the Vineyard of our Lord. Developing spiritual disciplines is to develop spiritual roots from which our faith can draw sap to grow strong and fruit-bearing branches. This Book explores Nine Spiritual Disciplines of the Kingdom of God.

These **Books** are available from: www.churchplantinginstitute.com or at www.amazon.com

Church Planting

How to plant a dynamic church

Dr. Hendrik J. Vorster

Foreword by: Dr. Yonggi Cho

Church Planting - Dr Hendrik J Vorster

Church Planting - How to plant a dynamic, disciple-making church

By Dr Hendrik J Vorster

This is a handbook for those who wish to plant a disciple-making church. This book explores every aspect of church planting, and is widely used in over 70 Nations on 6 Continents. Here is a list of the areas that are explored:

1. The challenge to plant New Churches
2. Phases of Church Planting
3. Phase One of Church Planting - The Calling, Vision and Preparation Phase
4. The Call to Church Planting
5. Twelve Characteristics of Church Planting Leaders
6. Church Planting Terminology
7. Phase Two of Church Planting - Discipleship
8. The Process of Discipleship
9. Phase Three of Church Planting - Congregating the Discipleship Groups
10. Understanding Church Planting Finances
11. Understanding Church staff
12. Phase Four of Church Planting - Ministry development and Church Launching Phase
13. Understanding and Implementing Systems
14. Phase Five of Church Planting - Multiplication
15. Understanding the challenges in Church Planting
16. How to succeed in Church Planting
17. How to plant a House Church

This Book, and Video Teaching materials, are available for purchase, from www.churchplantingcourses.com or through our website, www.churchplantinginstitute.com or at www.amazon.com

www.ingramcontent.com/pod-product-compliance
Lightning Source LLC
Chambersburg PA
CBHW060334050426
42449CB00011B/2751